D1165691

3 0900 00266 3368

Twayne's English Authors Series

EDITOR OF THIS VOLUME

Kinley Roby

Northeastern University

John Wain

TEAS 316

John Wain

JOHN WAIN

By DALE SALWAK

Citrus College

TWAYNE PUBLISHERS
A DIVISION OF G. K. HALL & CO., BOSTON

Copyright © 1981 by G. K. Hall & Co.

Published in 1981 by Twayne Publishers,
A Division of G. K. Hall & Co.
All Rights Reserved

Printed on permanent/durable acid-free paper and bound
in the United States of America

First Printing

Frontispiece photo of John Wain by D. Robertson

Library of Congress Cataloging in Publication Data

Salwak, Dale.
John Wain.

(Twayne's English authors ; TEAS, 316)
Bibliography: p. 142–51
Includes index.
1.   Wain, John—Criticism and interpretation.
PR6045.A249Z87   828′.914′09   80–22135
ISBN 0-8057-6806-8

For
Glenn and Betty

Contents

About the Author

Dale Salwak graduated with honors from Purdue University (1969) and received his M.A. (1970) and Ph.D. (1974) degrees in English Literature from the University of Southern California under a National Defense Education Act competitive fellowship program. As a faculty member of Southern California's Citrus College since 1973, Dale Salwak specializes in contemporary English and American literature, Advanced Composition, and Literature of the Bible. He is also the author of *Kingsley Amis: A Reference Guide* (1978) and *John Braine and John Wain: A Reference Guide* (1980), both published by G. K. Hall & Co. Currently he is editing a collection of interviews he conducted with Kingsley Amis, John Braine, John Wain, and Colin Wilson— to be published under the title *Literary Voices* (Borgo Press).

Preface

John Wain has an established reputation as an intelligent, learned man who is seriously concerned with the issues of his time and totally dedicated to the writer's craft. Over the past twenty-nine years, he has developed an impressive body of work in fiction, poetry, and criticism to become, as Richard Hoggart predicted, a modern man of letters.[1] He is the author of nine novels, three collections of short stories, eight volumes of verse, one autobiography, one biography, five volumes of criticism, six dramas, and many essays and reviews. Two of his works have merited distinguished literary recognition: Wain received the 1958 W. Somerset Maugham Award for *Preliminary Essays* and the James Tait Black Memorial Book prize in 1974 as well as the Whitbread Award in 1975 for *Samuel Johnson*. Writing in the *New Statesman*, John Raymond said concerning *Preliminary Essays*, "The great point about this book is that Mr. Wain cares intensely about literature and that he cares intelligently."[2] Of his *Samuel Johnson*, Edmund Fuller observed, "You will find no more 'grown-up' book, no deeper compassion and wisdom, no more edifying and ageless portrait in any work of this or many a season."[3]

Not all of his works have received such praise, nor should they have; but it is obvious from these and other assessments that Wain has already attained a position of consequence in contemporary English literature. It seems appropriate now—more than twenty-five years after the publication of his first novel—that the several scholarly articles which have dealt with his works be supplemented by a more inclusive, up-to-date study of all of his writings.

Because this is the first full-dress critique of the evolution of John Wain's career, I have chosen a strategy that is simple and direct: first a discussion of the relationship between Wain's life and work and a consideration of pertinent literary influences upon his writings; then a close reading of all of his novels in their order of publication; and finally an assessment of his other books—short stories, verse, and criticism—as they bear upon his longer fiction.

I should add that in examining the development of Wain's career I have tried to provide a focus which is not only central to his development as a literary artist but also honors the merits of each individual work. This method is both historical and descriptive, in evaluating his novels as part of a continuing literary tradition and as works of art in their own right. In each analysis, therefore, I have organized the material around the major areas of characterization, structure, and meaning.

Ideally, the reader of this book is someone who has already encountered the pleasures and difficulties of John Wain's works and wants to know more about them. At the same time, there are large numbers of people who, while fascinated by all they have heard about Wain from the 1950s on, have been reluctant to undertake the experience of actually reading his works, and I am hoping that this book will be useful to them as well: it is intended to enhance the understanding of those already familiar with his achievement, and encourage those new readers to appreciate the accomplishments of a modern man of letters.

In the writing of this book I have been generously helped, through both personal encouragement and professional advice, by Professors Stephen C. Moore and James W. Durbin at the University of Southern California; by Dr. Gordon N. Ray, President of the John Simon Guggenheim Memorial Foundation; and by my mother, Frances H. Salwak. To all of them I am very grateful.

I should also like to thank David Gerard, senior lecturer in the Department of Bibliographical Studies, College of Librarianship Wales, who was kind enough to answer my questions concerning bibliography; and the research librarians at the University of Southern California, the University of California at Los Angeles, and the University of Chicago for locating out-of-print materials.

Finally, my deepest gratitude must go to John Wain himself, who has written encouraging and informative letters to me about his life and his work as a novelist, poet, and critic.

DALE SALWAK

Citrus College

Acknowledgments

Acknowledgment is made to John Wain and to the following publishers for permission to quote from copyrighted works: to Curtis Brown, Ltd., for selections from *Hurry on Down* (1965) and *The Smaller Sky* (1967); to Viking Penguin, Inc. for selections from *A Winter in the Hills* (1970), and *The Pardoner's Tale* (1979); to St. Martin's Press, Inc., and Macmillan and Co., Ltd. for selections from *Strike the Father Dead* (1962) and *Sprightly Running* (1963).

Chronology

1925 John Barrington Wain born March 14 at No. 44 James Street, Stoke-on-Trent, Staffordshire — an industrial city.

1928 Moved to Penkhull, signaling a step up into the middle class.

1930 Attended a school run by the two daughters of the Vicar of Hartshill.

1931– Attended Froebel Preparatory School, Dresden
1934 (Longton).

1934– Attended Newcastle-under-Lyme High School, North
1942 Staffordshire.

1941 Joined the Officers Training Corps.

1943– Attended St. John's College, Oxford, B.A.
1946

1945 Founding editor of *Mandrake*.

1946– Fereday Fellow, St. John's College, Oxford, M.A. (1950).
1949

1947 Married Marianne Urmstom.

1947– Lecturer in English Literature, University of Reading,
1955 Berkshire.

1951 *Mixed Feelings: Nineteen Poems.*

1953 "First Readings" for BBC Third Programme; *Hurry on Down; Contemporary Reviews of Romantic Poetry* (ed.).

1954 *Hurry on Down* published as *Born in Captivity* in the United States.

1955 Resigned teaching post to become full-time writer; *Living in the Present; Interpretations: Essays on Twelve Poems* (ed.).

1956 Divorced; *A Word Carved on a Sill.*

1957 *Preliminary Essays.*

1958 *The Contenders; International Literary Annual* (ed.); received the W. Somerset Maugham Award for *Preliminary Essays.*

1958–1959	Transferred to the MacDowell Colony, New Hampshire, then to New York, Brooklyn Heights—where his neighbors included Truman Capote and Norman Mailer.
1959	*A Travelling Woman; Gerard Manley Hopkins: An Idiom of Desperation.*
1960	Fellow, Royal Society of Literature (resigned, 1961); *Living in the Present* reissued in the United States; married Eirian James; *Nuncle and Other Stories.*
1961	*Fanny Burney's Diary* (ed.); director, Poetry Book Society Festival, "Poetry of the Mermaid," London; *Weep Before God: Poems; A Song About Major Eatherly.*
1962	*Sprightly Running: Part of an Autobiography; Strike the Father Dead.*
1963	*Anthology of Modern Poetry* (ed.); *Pope* (ed.); *The Take-Over Bid* (radio drama).
1964	*The Living World of Shakespeare: A Playgoer's Guide.*
1965	*The Young Visitors; Wildtrack: A Poem.*
1966	*Death of the Hind Legs and Other Stories; Selected Shorter Poems of Thomas Hardy* (ed.); *Selected Stories of Thomas Hardy* (ed.); *The Dynasts* (ed.).
1967	Churchill Visiting Professor, University of Bristol; *The Smaller Sky; Arnold Bennett; The Young Visitors* (television drama).
1968	*Shakespeare: Macbeth: A Casebook* (ed.).
1969	Visiting professor, Centre Universitaire Experimental, Vincennes, France; *Letters to Five Artists.*
1970	*A Winter in the Hills.*
1971	*The Life Guard and Other Stories; Shakespeare: Othello: A Casebook* (ed.); first holder, Fellowship in Creative Arts, Brasenose College, Oxford.
1972	*A House for the Truth: Critical Essays; The Shape of Feng.*
1973	*Johnson as Critic* (ed.); elected professor of Poetry, Oxford.
1974	*Dr. Johnson Out of Town* (radio drama); *Samuel Johnson,* for which he received the James Tait Black Memorial Book Prize.
1975	*Harry in the Night: An Optimistic Comedy* (stage drama); *Feng: A Poem; Samuel Johnson: Lives of the English Poets: A Selection* (ed.); received the Whitbread Award for *Samuel Johnson.*

1976   *Johnson on Johnson: A Selection of the Personal and Autobiographical Writings of Samuel Johnson: 1709-1784* (ed.); *Assassination* (radio drama).
1977   *Professing Poetry.*
1978   *Personal Choice: A Poetry Anthology* (ed); *The Pardoner's Tale; The New Wessex Selection of Thomas Hardy's Poetry* (edited with Eirian Wain); *You Wouldn't Remember* (radio drama); *An Edmund Wilson Celebration* (ed.), also published in the United States as *Edmund Wilson: The Man and His Work; Hurry on Down* reissued with an introduction by the author.
1979   *Anthology of Contemporary Poetry* (ed.).
1980   *Poems: 1949-1979; Samuel Johnson* reissued with an added preface.

CHAPTER 1

The Man

A S novelist, poet, and critic, John Wain has been described as a "painfully honest" writer who is always, to an unusual degree, writing autobiography.[1] His own fortunes and his emotional reactions to these fortunes are, of course, transformed in various ways. His purpose is artistic, not confessional, and he shapes his material accordingly. As Wain himself states, this intention is both pure and simple: to express his own feelings honestly and to tell the truth about the world he knows. Particularly in his fiction, Wain finds a great many ways to convey the message that life is ultimately tragic. Human beings suffer; life is difficult; the comic mask conceals anguish. Only occasionally is this grim picture relieved by some sort of idealism, some unexpected attitude of unselfishness or tenderness. What is more, in all of his writings we find evidence of a thoughtful, literate man coming to terms with these truths in a sincere and forthright manner.

Although his world is the twentieth century, Wain is very much an eighteenth-century man who defends—as did his "moral hero,"[2] Samuel Johnson—the value of reason, moderation, common sense, moral courage, and intellectual self-respect. He delights in pointing out that he and Johnson were born in the same district ("The Potteries") and in much the same social milieu; that he attended the same University as Johnson (Oxford); that he has known, like Johnson, the Grub Street experience and "the unremitting struggle to write enduring books against the background of an unstable existence."[3] What chiefly interests the critic in surveying Wain's formative years are the reasons for his increasingly somber outlook. One of Wain's books—an autobiography entitled *Sprightly Running* (1962)—remains the best account of his formative years as well as one of the most engaging statements of many of his opinions. In it we find some of the profound and lasting effects on his writing rooted in his childhood, his adolescence, and his years at Oxford University and afterwards.

I   The Early Years: 1925–1943

John Barrington Wain was born on March 14, 1925, in Stoke-on-Trent, Staffordshire, an industrial city given over to pottery and coal-mining. As Wain explains, the six towns that make up its amalgamation lie end to end along the valley of the Trent. Most of the residential districts are up on the high ground at the crest of the valley on either side; most of the humbler dwellings, in the valley. Here, as in other English cities, a move upward in social status is signaled by a move up in geographical terms. Therefore, the Wain family's move three years later to Penkhull—a manufacturing complex of kilns and factories and, incidentally, the setting for his third novel, *The Contenders*—marked a step up into the middle-class district where most of the population was working-class.

The people he knew during these formative years were "hard-working, forthright, kindly and blessed with an earthy sense of humour."[4] His father, Arnold A. Wain—"an exceptionally energetic and capable man"[5]—worked his way up from "barefoot poverty" to establish a modestly successful dentist practice. His mother, Anne Turner, was "a gentle and responsive person" (p. 58), but rather timid and anxious. Wain adds that there was a good pipeline to the working class, too, through the side of the family that had not risen in the world, but had remained what the Wains for generations had been, artisans. Although the family was not particularly academic-oriented, they "always had plenty of discussion of general ideas, . . . the house was well stocked with books" (p. 163), and his family experiences were quite educative. The circumstances of his childhood and adolescence in fact were uniquely valuable in his growth as a writer; without them, Wain would have been not only different but diminished. These circumstances centered on four areas: the dwindling countryside, the advancing industrialism, the threatened minority, and his early writings and readings.

From infancy, Wain had a genuine fondness for the countryside. He immersed himself in the sights and sounds and colors of rural nature, all of which made an impression on him that was distinctive as well as deep. He traces his kinship with a disappearing English "nature" to the days when he loved having his pram wheeled under the trees. There he would sit for hours looking at the opposite slope of the valley. A gamekeeper's cottage captured his imagination. "It simply stood there as a symbol," he writes, "a symbol of that pastoral landscape for which I seemed to have been born with a craving" (p. 2). This craving developed into "a deep, unargued reverence for all created life, almost a pantheism" (p. 35). Stuffy rooms, heavy clothes, revolted him—anything that helped "to make human life one degree more 'unnatural' " (p. 32).

On holidays he and his family traveled to the coast and hills of North Wales—an association which carried over into his adult years when, at thirty-four, he married a Welsh woman. His feeling for Wales—for the independent life of the people, the landscape and mountains, the sea, the special light of the sun—is recorded in *A Winter in the Hills.* Strongly presented in this novel and others is the idea that nature is the embodiment of order, permanence, and life. Indeed, the tension between the nightmare of repression in society and the dream of liberation in the natural world is an important unifying theme throughout his entire body of work. And from his retrospective account it is evident that Wain prefers the countryside to the town—"in every way, including morally" (p. 32). In these early experiences we find the child who, in his innocence and freshness, is more open to the beauty of nature, more susceptible to its influence. So it was in his own youth, and, happily, so it has continued to be as he has grown older.

The experience of living in an industrial town also left an indelible imprint upon Wain's mind and his art. His exposure to the lives of the working class and to the advance of industrialism gave him a profound knowledge of the working people and their problems, all of which he depicts with sympathy and humanity in his fiction. Wain was always a sensitive child; under the circumstances, it would have been hard for a sensitive child not to be attentive to the grimmer aspects of the world about him. The Sutton—a housing estate for slum clearance in the valley— gave him "the perpetual sense of living in a beleaguered garrison" (p. 4). The scene was for Wain a visual menace:

"Hedges were slashed; trees had their branches torn off and their bark carved and stripped away; every pool where a few sticklebacks had managed to breed was swept by a thousand nets until the last survivor had been carried away to die in a stifling jam-jar" (p. 4). From his early comic fiction to his most somber novel, *The Pardoner's Tale,* the persecution of the minority and the crumbling away of dignity and decency are among his most important fictional themes.

Moreover, Wain's experiences at Froebel's Preparatory School and at Newcastle-under-Lyme High School impressed on him the idea that life was competitive and "a perpetual effort to survive" (p. 22). He found himself surrounded and outnumbered by people who resented him for being different from themselves. Perhaps the source of this resentment was that he dressed better, lived in a bigger house with servants, or had parents who drove him to school each morning. Wain reminds us that houses in Penkhull were often suspected of being snobbish, and Wain had to prove continually that he was not. In any event, Wain acquired a certain defensiveness in a world in which he found himself, at best, only tolerated. His contact with older children, schoolboy bullies, and authoritative schoolmasters taught Wain three vital lessons: "(1) that the world was dangerous; (2) that it was not possible to evade these dangers by being inoffensive, since [he] was surrounded on all sides by those who hated [him], . . .; (3) that, although the natural reaction to all this was fear, [he] could not admit to feeling fear or [he] should be disgraced" (p. 6). These "lessons of life" carried over into his works giving him the habit of identifying himself with the "threatened minority." We find in his fiction, for instance, a sense of the difficulty of survival in an intrusive and demanding world. The worst of characters is always the bully, and the worst of societies is always totalitarian. Wain explains that a scene from his first novel, *Hurry on Down* (written between 1949 and 1952), contains at its center a mood born one afternoon in 1935 when a gang of schoolboys bullied and beat him:

As I scrambled to my feet, dazed, nursing my knee, and saw, on the one hand, the glowering faces of the elementary-school boys, and on the other the aloof backs of my schoolfellows . . . [I] wondered how, between the two of them, I was ever going to find a place to live. (p. 62)

The competitive spirit Wain discovered in the English school system also becomes a theme in *The Contenders*. This training demands such intense competition that the heroes, Robert Lamb and Ned Roper, are marked by it, spending their entire lives pursuing goals the inherent value of which they never question. While the public schools resolved the difficulty of obtaining an education, these institutions, as Wain depicts them, simply impeded rather than aided his education.

It is not at all surprising, therefore, that the use and abuse of power plays so prominent a part in Wain's thought. From his schooldays Wain came to understand very well and experience intensely the ruthless exercise of power, the manipulation of the law, and the whole system of reward and punishment, conformity and dissent. Ever since, he recalls,

I [have been able] to enter imaginatively into the world of any modern dictatorship, simply by seeing it as a school-world inhabited by adults, and with everything sealed up accordingly—real guns instead of toy ones, real beatings and killings instead of token ones. But the same atmosphere of treacheries and loyalties, the same feeling that power, the naked lust to dominate, is the mainspring of life. (p. 24)

Beginning with *Hurry on Down*, each of Wain's published novels and stories is concerned in some way with the power and control that some people can have over others.

To cope with these injustices as well as with his own fears and inadequacies during the early years, Wain turned to humor, debate, and music. He discovered his verbal quickness, and with it, his wit, so that he grew into a " 'character,' one of the school notabilities, able to break conventions and get away with it, tolerated and even, within strict limits, admired" (p. 69). The human race, Wain implies, for all its grotesqueries, absurdities, and shams, has one really effective surgeon—laughter. Power, money, persuasion, and persecution are small weapons by comparison. Against the assault of laughter nothing can stand. For Wain, the humorist is above all else a moralist, in whose hands the ultimate weapon of laughter might conceivably become the means of liberating mankind from its enslavement to false ideals. Thus his mimicry of both authorities and students was used as the quickest way of convincing one that something was horrible or boring or absurd. In both *Hurry on Down* and *The Contenders*, for example, the heroes use mockery and ridicule to cope with their unjust world.

Besides a lively sense of humor and a zest for debate, Wain early developed another interest which has colored his personal and literary development—his interest in jazz. He has spoken and written often of his lifelong enthusiasm for the trumpet playing of Bill Coleman. And he admits that Percy Brett, the black jazz musician in *Strike the Father Dead*, was created with Coleman in mind. Years later, after he had met Coleman and they had become good friends, Wain dedicated a poem to the man and his music in *Letters to Five Artists*. Wain's deep feelings for traditional jazz may have begun as another means of escape from the pressures of school, but certainly it provided him with experiences from which he would draw material for his later fiction and verse.

Accompanying these early experiences was a growing interest in serious writing and reading—two additional ingredients in the personality of the later artist. Unlike many youths, Wain did not have to endure the agonizing doubt and indecision of trying to decide what he wanted to do and what part in life he was fitted to play. By the age of nine, he knew: he wanted to be an author. But his earliest literary efforts were more critical than imaginative; not until his middle twenties did his desire to be a creative writer fully emerge. Therefore, he began as a critically conscious writer who delighted in "pastiche and parody for their own sake" (p. 164). He began routinely to write novels in his exercise books, novels which focused on a private eye named Swellum Owte and which parodied his own readings. Then, as now, he found most difficult the task of maintaining a steady plot line. Particularly noteworthy was his large vocabulary. He recognizes that these early writings represent a bent transferred to criticism in the best known of his later critical studies.

Wain matched such voracious writing with almost equally voracious reading of prose and verse. Wain himself has cited his family's liking for books as a significant fact of his youth. His wide reading at home of such books as *Tom Brown's Schooldays*, *Oliver Twist*, and *Tom Sawyer* he supplemented by frequent trips to the local library. Wain's early interest in these classics, together with those by Dickens, Smollett, Defoe, and others, influenced his later literary style. In common with these writers, the structure of Wain's novels is direct and chronological, he approaches his characters through the conventional narration of the realist, and his concerns are social and moral.

But Wain's reading was not limited to fiction, for by the age of fourteen he discovered poetry. The first poet to make an impact on him was Shakespeare, whose "verse seemed to jump off the page to [him] and flood [his] mind with an extraordinary joy."[6] He found that certain lines put him into "a state of exultation that was almost trance-like."[7] He devoured the English poets—from Shakespeare to the Romantics, from the Victorians to the moderns, then back to the seventeenth century. At the same time he applied himself to serious study of French and Latin, because "[he] wanted to see what their poets were like."[8] In other words, Wain had entered into that life which he continues to lead today—the life of a man of letters.

The provinces, industrialism, class lines, school competitiveness, music, and literature—these are some of the major childhood influences on Wain's personality and, consequently, his art. It may well be that Wain's attitude to the working people and their world, with its special compassion and understanding, was partly derived from these early experiences. He clearly thinks so. *Hurry on Down, Living in the Present,* and *A Winter in the Hills*—not to mention many of his short stories—are expressions of the resentment, the guilt, and the stinging pity for those pinned to the earth by the system that one would expect to see engendered by these means in a young man whose mind was both strong and sensitive. But whatever evil he endured, some good came of it: far from growing into a timid, insecure man, Wain proved notably self-reliant as he undertook the grueling life of a man of letters. He matured decidedly early in many ways and feels grateful that those years in school gave him, at least, "a tough, shared local root that nothing can now pull up" (p. 74).

II   *The University Years: 1943–1955*

The second major period in Wain's life occurred between 1943, when he entered St. John's College, Oxford, and 1955, when he resigned his post as lecturer in English at Reading University to become a full-time writer. This is the period in which he grew, with remarkable speed, into the world of literature and scholarship. At St. John's he shaped his identity as a writer: the books were there to be read, and the learned men were there to talk with. As was to be so often the case, Wain found strength in his work. When life seemed to be crumbling about him, he found new motivation from usefulness and productive work, from the sense that he had skills and knowledge that were needed and so could respect himself. Along with his studies, Wain drew deep nourishment from personal contact with artists of every kind. To be an artist means accepting insecurity, being a target for criticism, some of it wounding. Wain admits that, in his own life, "courage would have failed, many a time, but for the companionship of people who had made the same decision, who spend their lives *making things.*"[9]

This nourishment and companionship came from many sources. At Oxford, for example, hours of reading helped to lay the foundation of his intimate, lifelong familiarity with Samuel Johnson. In this eighteenth-century writer Wain found reflected his own "sense of stoical resistance against hopeless odds" (p. 101), and he collected every book by or about the man that he could find. This collection included a 1765 edition of Johnson's *Dictionary,* which he bought in 1943 and "trundled back to [his] college room on a handcart."[10] The dictionary, he asserts, "has made the greatest single contribution to such understanding of eighteenth-century life and literature as I have attained."[11]

Also sustaining to Wain were friends he might talk with and learn from—friends of penetration and sensitivity. He found himself surrounded and his life enriched by older men in whom, however improbably, he discerned embodiments of Johnson. These associates included C. S. Lewis (his tutor) and the remarkable Charles Williams, both of whom made a serious effort to train Wain's mind. From Lewis, he learned to express himself precisely; his quickness in debate was "a wonderful example and a wonderful stimulus"[12] to the young Wain. He learned his lessons well. His literary criticism is intelligent and perceptive; he analyzes and explains what he sees clearly and cogently. What he learned as a critic influenced his fiction, too. In his imaginative writings, some of his attitudes and points of view are explained and documented with significant and contemporary details.

If Lewis's literary attitudes helped to shape Wain's critical acumen, Charles Williams's poetic spirit helped to encourage

Wain's love of verse. Great poetry, Williams taught, is "a triumph of the human spirit and should be approached with joy and gratitude" (p. 150). Wain adds:

That I remained deeply conscious of the debt that the rest of us owe to any man who has been through the furnace and emerged as an artist . . . is as much Williams's doing as anyone's. (p. 151).

Williams was "generous, free of malice, too much absorbed in contemplation of great writing and greater revelation to stoop to petty self-seeking" (p. 151). He was always willing to praise a man for what he genuinely did well. Wain's additional comments on Williams could readily apply to Wain himself: he was "a lover and praiser" (p. 150); he was one whose "mood never seemed to fall below the level of blazing enthusiasm. Great poetry was something to be revelled in, to be rejoiced over" (p. 149). Undoubtedly, Williams's encouragement and friendly criticism at this time stimulated the younger man to write and to consider more closely the kind of poetry he wished to write; moreover, Williams's influence is evident in Wain's later essays, notably those collected in *Professing Poetry,* in which we find his preference for a reverential posture: poetry is to be admired, not judged.

Two friends made in his Oxford period especially influenced his writing. One was Philip Larkin, in whom Wain sensed "a rock-like determination to do whatever it might be necessary to do in order to write well" (p. 188). Had this meeting never occurred, Wain admits, "my life would have been the poorer, for his personal example has always been one of the greatest importance to me" (p. 187). Wain was also influenced by another friend made in his Oxford career—Kingsley Amis. Because Amis seemed to be having so much fun writing *The Legacy,* Wain himself sat down to try to write a novel. "Amis's example was certainly one of [Wain's] motives" (p. 204). He continues:

[Amis] had made it seem . . . simple and natural to be trying to shape one's day-to-day reaction to life into fiction. I'm quite certain I would never have written *Hurry on Down* without the example of that first, undergraduate novel of Amis's. (p. 204)

The years of contact with Larkin and Amis represented a period of inspiration for Wain. The dedication of *Mixed Feelings*—his first important creative work—suggests his gratitude to Amis as a catalyst for later productivity. Oxford and the period of time spent there unquestionably and understandably have meant much to Wain.

After completing his formal education in 1950, Wain accepted a full-time position as lecturer in English Literature at Reading University. Initially, at least, this period as a lecturer contributed to his writing, for here, as at Oxford, he was surrounded by people who helped him, encouraged him, and educated him. At the same time, Wain continued to pursue his writing career. He employed odds and ends of time to develop his first novel, not particularly because he wished to be a novelist, but to see if he could write one that would get into print. In 1953, Frederick Warburg bought *Hurry on Down,* and the unexpected success quickly established Wain's reputation as one of Britain's promising new writers.

However, the exhilarating experience with his first book was poor preparation for the sobering slump that followed. Beginning in 1953, Wain suffered through one of the worst periods of his life. Ill health, later divorce proceedings, and the drudgery of a scholar's life pushed him into a bad crisis of depression and discouragement: not only about himself, but also about the society in which he was living. He tried to climb out of this crisis by leaving the university for a year and retreating to the Swiss Alps. There he let his imagination loose on his own problems. The result was *Living in the Present,* a depressing book of manifest despair and disgust. The tone of the novel is that of a man forcing himself to write (he admits to having been pressured by the publisher to write another novel after his initial success), and it was neither an artistic nor a financial success. However, out of this period in Wain's life developed a profound awareness about love and loneliness, union and estrangement. As we shall see, the essential loneliness of human beings, and their more or less successful attempts to overcome this loneliness by love, become major themes in his later fiction.

In December 1955, Wain resigned his post as lecturer because he found it increasingly difficult to work both as an academic and as a writer. "I left teaching because I wanted to write," he says in his autobiography, "not merely because I didn't want to teach" (p. 173). But he looks back upon his university years as richly rewarding ones because they gave him "a profession, an orientation, a circle of friends which [he still has], and—less definably—the sense of belonging to a clerisy and sharing its responsibilities and ideals."[13] In the course of his readings and talks, he grew sensitive to the ingredients that go into making a literary work and, what is more, into valuing the aesthetic pleasure and emotional satisfaction it affords the reader. More important, he came to value literature for its involvement in the world, what it can tell us about ourselves and one another, what it can do for us in helping us to live our own lives. With that in mind as his purpose in life, he has since 1955 devoted himself full-time to his writing.

As the following chapters will indicate, Wain's writing is directly related to his experience. In his novels and stories he is engaged in a searching examination of the contemporary social scene in England, with a negative conclusion. The world he surveys is fraught with perils and profoundly contemptuous of human needs. His earlier works, up to and including *The Contenders,* reflect his personal struggle: the normal rebellious feelings of a spirited and intelligent schoolboy, forced against his will into an obsolete pattern of governing-class values in an unjust world; the harmful effects of his early years in turning away from vital involvement with life; and the compensating force and steadiness of his love of the provinces, respect for the dignity of the individual man, and compassion for the under-privileged. Starting as a misfit adolescent, he gradually grew into the knowledge that the strength had been given him to push ahead step by step; by the time he resigned his lecturer post at Reading University, he had proven his ability to survive. This knowledge permeates *Strike the Father Dead.* The later writing—everything, more or less, from *The Young Visitors* onward—reflects Wain's concern with the effects of loneliness and the remoteness of love. Thematically the novels show a marked increase in the treatment of various social corruptions and evils, and the fiction is constructed around one or the other of two possible responses to that world. One is an attitude involving submission to tragic realities. The second countenances what might be thought of as a strategic retreat from the circumstances of tragedy. *A Winter in the Hills* is full in the mainstream of this later period of Wain's writings. Here, and in everything that follows, the first thing we notice is that the knockabout element is completely banished. The tone of the later writing is grave, dignified, and compassionate, reflecting his natural propensity to look on the dark side of life.

III   The "Angry Young Man" Decade

To understand something of the British literary climate that helped to shape Wain's novels, we must go back at least to the end of World War II. For about ten years after the war, the older established writers continued to produce. Men such as Aldous Huxley, Graham Greene, Evelyn Waugh, C. P. Snow, and Anthony Powell had made their reputations before the war and continued to be the major literary voices at this time. Most of them had been educated in public schools, then by Oxford or Cambridge, and were from upper- or upper-middle-class origins. Their novels were likely to center around fashionable London or some country estate. Often they confined their satire to the intellectual life and the cultural as well as social predicaments of the upper middle class.

However, a combination of events led to the appearance of another "group" of writers. Within a period of three years, several new and accomplished writers ushered in a fresh generation whose central thematic concerns and stylistic vigor altered the traditions and practices of prewar British fiction. These writers, including Wain, Amis, John Braine, John Osborne, Angus Wilson, and Alan Sillitoe, turned away from technical innovations, complexity, and the sensitive, introspective protagonist to concentrate on concrete problems of current society, in its cultural and social aspects. Because these writers seemed to express similar concerns, and because many came from working- or lower-middle-class backgrounds, went to Oxford or Cambridge, and taught for a time at a provincial university, journalists soon spoke of them as belonging to a literary movement called "the Angry Young Men"—an epithet suggesting writers of social protest or critics of man's plight in the modern world. Their works shared a commonality of theme and style: (1) resentment of a rigid class stratification; (2) rejection of formal institutional ties and relationships; (3) discouragement with economic insecurities and low status of those without money; (4) loathing of pretentiousness in any form; (5) disenchantment with the past; and (6) unadorned use of everyday language.

Very different, too, is the kind of hero they created. He is essentially the "antihero," the man who is at the mercy of life. Although sometimes capable of aspiration and thought, he is not strong enough to carve out his destiny in the way he wishes. Frequently, he is something of a dreamer, tossed about by life, and also pushed about, or at least overshadowed, by the threats in his life. Wain's Charles Lumley and Edgar Banks, Amis's Jim Dixon, Braine's Joe Lampton, and Sillitoe's Arthur Seaton all bear the marks of this type. Often there is discernible in their characters a modern malaise, a vague discontent, and a yearning for some person or set of circumstances beyond their reach. Sometimes, the sense of disenchantment with life as it is becomes so great that the individual expresses a desire not to live at all, as Edgar Banks asserts in *Living in the Present* and as Gus Howkins declares in *The Pardoner's Tale*.

Along with the contemporary antihero, much of the newer fiction reflects interest in eighteenth-century novels. The young writers found that novelists like Smollett, for example, who used farce for a serious purpose, were much more interesting. So they started to write like that again. In their humor, episodic plot, and unpretentious style, Wain's first few novels remind us of the traditional picaresque tale. His early heroes are often rogues, more shrewd than perceptive, interested more in creature comforts than in the arts, opportunistic and pragmatic rather than idealistic. We may view this return to the picaresque novel as a definite reaction against the complex experimental novels of James Joyce or Virginia Woolf. The fumbling antihero is an apt spokesman for the post-Romantic, post-Freudian age, which, having witnessed an economic depression and several wars, has rediscovered the fact of man's limitation. Also, the novels are good entertainment, providing comic relief for a reading public weary of tormented, alienated artists and tired of despairing about the future of a world seemingly bent on self-destruction.[14]

To many members of the Establishment, however, these young writers were educated men who didn't want to be gentlemen: "a new rootless, faithless, classless class" lacking in manners and morals.[15] W. Somerset Maugham called them "mean, malicious and envious . . . scum,"[16] and warned that these men would some day rule England. Wain was widely represented by the press as one of the group's leading and most controversial figures.

Nevertheless, other literary journalists considered the new

writers to represent a refreshing change in the development of British fiction. To some journalists, *Hurry on Down* was a fairly reliable mirror of the mood of its day, with its documentation of contemporary history, its illustration of social changes, the effect of the Welfare State, and the dangers of widespread education. They pointed out that although Charles Lumley is indeed angry, his anger is not of the same quality or intensity as that of Sillitoe's or Osborne's heroes. Arthur Seaton (in *Saturday Night and Sunday Morning*) is an angry young worker who escapes from his factory job on weekends by taking women to bed and by going on drunken sprees. Jimmy Porter (in *Look Back in Anger*), who some feel to be the archetypal angry young man and to whom critics originally applied the term, rages against a world in which nothing is very important. Its setting is the 1950s; its subject is the crisis in social values that were changing English society. Porter has a university education, but he is enraged by the middle-class values he would have to adopt to get a "good" job. Instead, he maintains a market stall in a provincial town where he vents his anger on all who come near him. His frustration reveals the plight of the newly educated poor, who both respected and derided the ethics of the privileged classes.

On the other hand, in *A Room at the Top* John Braine examined the personal crises which attend a shift in social position. Joe Lampton has the characteristic social background, but unlike the other "angry" heroes, he knows that he wants to reach the top of society. The novel illustrates the difficulties and hazards of the slow rise to the top, for in the process Lampton destroys the integrity of both himself and his personal relationships.

Kingsley Amis's *Lucky Jim* is closest in spirit to *Hurry on Down*. Like Lumley, Jim Dixon is a man educated in a Red Brick university, irreverent toward some of the traditions of the British Establishment, and impatient with the hypocrisy of the bourgeoisie. Amis's early heroes rebel against the academic racket by mocking it. Like Lumley, Dixon's aim is not to reform but to escape the values and the class system of society by remaining aloof and hence neutral.

Since the 1950s, the angry young men have moved so far from one another that few critical generalizations truly apply to them. The most we can say is that they favor clarity, honesty, and reason in their fiction and verse, and that they distrust excessive emotion and technical experimentation. Certainly, too, they all represent broadly similar social and educational backgrounds, and they embrace a reading public extending beyond the limits of that background. But since the publication of their works which gave rise to the label "the Angry Young Men," these writers have developed in different directions.[17]

Although Wain is aware of the publicity value that talk of a "school" makes possible, he rejects the term and refuses to be linked closely to the other writers. He views the angry young men as a " 'put-up job by non-writing journalists in an attempt to make writers interesting enough for gossip columns.' "[18] He rightly believes that his writing displays peculiar features resistant to categorization and that such identification tends to blur his characteristic qualities as a writer and literary personality. Putting labels behind him, his interest is in expressing his reactions to life in words. "My medium is not the novel, or the poem, or the play, or the short story: it is the vocabulary. And the decision as to which form to mould the words into must be a decision of the moment" (p. 202). Although literary journalists continue to link Wain with all sorts of writers, the only link that makes any sense at all is the identification with Amis, with whom Wain has been compared both favorably and unfavorably. Wain says, however, that between the two of them there is a fundamental contrast in outlook:

My vision of life is more extreme than his, both darker and brighter; his work is based on a steadying common sense, a real hatred of imbalance and excess; mine, by comparison, is apocalyptic. (p. 205)

Moreover, though Wain can at times match Amis's humor, Wain reveals in his fiction and verse a much greater tolerance for human weakness, a much greater tendency to pity the weak and erring even while exposing their errors, than Amis has ever shown in either his fiction or his verse.

We have seen that many of the circumstances of John Wain's formative years contributed to his darker vision of life. Yet possibly the deepest causes of Wain's pessimism lie in his own disposition. Like many artists, he was shy as a child, acutely sensitive, diffident. Such a nature ensured that he was more acutely wounded by the sorrows and disappointments of life than a coarser individual would have been. Near the end to *Sprightly*

Running, Wain reflects on his fundamental pessimism, and his comments surely reflect on his fiction:

To me, life is tragic, because humanity is made up of contradictions. . . . Each of us wants contradictory things, and some of our hopes will come to nothing, some of our powers will lie idle, whatever we do. We can never follow up all the possibilities that life indicates to us: if we try to, we destroy ourselves, and if we choose one path and follow it resolutely, we hanker inwardly after the paths we have neglected. . . . What is worse, every happiness can boomerang into suffering. To take joy in loving is to invite the agony that will follow when the loved one is taken away. To fasten your affection on anything or anyone is to lay your head on the block. (p. 260)

Wain's insistence on the contradictions of life is at the very center of his works, and is itself a tacit recommendation to us to look with honesty at the reality around us. For Wain, writing seems almost a test of his own honesty, to remind himself that, for the most part, we can look at things squarely, without flinching and without telling lies. And this stoic honesty, first to appear in embryo in *Hurry on Down,* becomes probably the single most dominant impression emerging from his work. Add to that, of course, a gentleness, or quiet caring, toward his treatment of people, and we have the portrait of a man who from the 1950s has become more seriously, deeply, and intelligently the critic of contemporary English society. "I hope my work is taking on a deeper note," he commented once; "otherwise there's no point in going on."[19]

CHAPTER 2

A Comic World

IN his first four novels—*Hurry on Down* (1953), *Living in the Present* (1955), *The Contenders* (1958), and *A Travelling Woman* (1959)—Wain comically perceives the difficulties of surviving in a demanding, sometimes fearful world. Detached from political causes and progress of their own lives, Wain's early heroes are drifters, seeking to compromise with or to escape from such "evils" as class lines, boredom, hypocrisy, and the conventional perils of success. Ultimately, each hero makes an effort to preserve himself. Charles Lumley (*Hurry on Down*) actively rebels by assuming a variety of personae. Edgar Banks (*Living in the Present*) resolves to kill himself and to take one despicable soul with him. Joe Shaw (*The Contenders*) recalls the history of Robert Lamb and Ned Roper, both of whom are dehumanized by their struggle for success. George Links (*A Travelling Woman*) turns to adultery in an attempt to relieve his boredom. However, each character compromises at the end. Lumley becomes a comedy writer. Banks retreats to his original job. Shaw returns to London; and Links tries to rejoin his wife. Although each novel carries a serious moral interest, Wain's wit, sharp observations, and inventiveness keep the plot moving. His comedy exaggerates, reforms, and criticizes to advocate the reasonable in social behavior and to promote the value and dignity of the individual.

I Hurry on Down

Like Kingsley Amis's *Lucky Jim*, John Braine's *Room at the Top*, and Alan Sillitoe's *Saturday Night and Sunday Morning*, Wain's first novel probes tellingly into a central problem of the 1950s. Its hero—Charles Lumley—is a creation of the postwar British Welfare State. As a discontented youth on his own for the first time, he feels that neither his upbringing nor his university education has prepared him for making a satisfactory living. Because he has a driving obsession to avoid the phony in life, he detests the world he sees and rebels against whatever is bourgeois and commonplace.

The plot of *Hurry on Down* reminds us of the traditional picaresque adventure story: (1) a series of short and often comic adventures loosely strung together; (2) an opportunistic and pragmatic hero who seeks to make a living through his wits; and (3) a prominence of satire on various English character types. As the novel opens, Lumley's landlady suspects that he has no job prospects; therefore, she is worried about his inability to pay his rent. Seeking a remedy, Lumley decides to visit his fiancée, Sheila. He arrives at her home but learns she is away. Instead, Edith Tharkles, her sister, is there with her stuffy husband, Robert. Both treat Lumley with hostility. In turn, he insults them, showers them with greasy water, gets drunk in a pub, and becomes sick. Having revenged himself against the Tharkles, Lumley is now ready for a different way of life.

Throughout his wanderings, Lumley maintains that his aim is to escape all identification with class. Ironically, each of his jobs is involved with society and carries some sort of class identification. His first position, for example, is as a window cleaner. He rents an apartment in an old building where he lives with Edwin Froulish, a self-advertising pseudo-Modernist writer, and Betty, a slatternly prostitute who supports Froulish. When this situation fails to satisfy him, Lumley resigns from his job as window cleaner and accepts a position as an expert delivery driver. He finds himself partners with Ern Ollershaw without knowing much about his background. Complications develop as Lumley meets and falls in love with Veronica, unaware that she is the mistress of wealthy Mr. Roderick. If Lumley is to have her, he will have to earn more money.

Shortly thereafter, Ollershaw is arrested for taking part in a car-theft racket. Because of his association with Ollershaw, Lumley becomes involved in the complicated liaisons of the racket and narrowly escapes being killed. Ultimately, he ends up in a hospital, where he learns the truth about Veronica. Under the hospital's care, Lumley is nursed back to health and becomes a hospital orderly. He takes up with Rosa, a pleasant but rather simple-minded girl, and for a short time he believes he will marry her. Later, however, he comes to recognize that their interests are too far apart. Through a series of fortunate circumstances, Lumley meets Mr. Braceweight, a millionaire, and goes to work as his chauffeur. The new tutor for Braceweight's son is George Hutchins, a former classmate of Lumley. The two do not get along well, and Hutchins contributes to Lumley's departure from the scene.

Lumley's next position is as a bouncer in a night club. When this, too, proves unsuitable for his tastes, he becomes a comedy writer for a radio show—a job he considers neutral with respect to class. At this point in the narrative, Veronica appears. Lumley still loves her, but he recognizes that she is the form that his new captivity will take. She will be his new cage. By the end of the novel, he realizes that the individual and his own values are more important than any badges of class. Ironically, he learns this in the midst of a highly organized and commercial world as a gag writer. He settles, finally, for the girl he always had wanted (and could not get) and a modest "pot of gold" through the help of Mr. Roderick.

When the novel was published in England in 1953, the general agreement among early critics was that Wain had produced an impressive first novel. It was praised in the *Spectator* for being "inventive, impulsive, cogitative and often very funny."[1] J. B. Priestley in the London *Sunday Times* liked it "for its brave attempt at the picaresque."[2] Walter Allen, who saw in Wain the makings of a true satirist, linked Lumley and Jim Dixon as exponents of "the new hero."[3] When the novel was published in the United States as *Born in Captivity* a year later, Dan Wickendon in the *New York Herald Tribune Book Review* said that Wain's "sinewy prose, full of strong verbs and fresh witty images, is a joy to read."[4] The *New Yorker* called it "a bright, wry, intelligent, and generally amusing book."[5]

But not all the reviewers were as impressed with the novel as these excerpts indicate. The *Manchester Guardian* reviewer felt that although Wain was well equipped for modern comedy, "his moods do not mix comfortably."[6] The *Times Literary Supplement* found the novel to be rather "clumsy in conception."[7] Edmund Fuller, writing in the *New York Times Book Review*, called the book unsatisfactory because Wain apparently failed to decide what *kind* of book he was writing.[8] George Scott in *Truth* suggested that perhaps the picaresque convention forced Wain to give "but a superficial impression of the modern background to his comedy."[9] To Anthony Burgess, the novel was ill constructed and written in an "indifferent style."[10] He recommended that Wain give up novel-writing and continue to produce short stories, in which he demonstrated a more consistent control.

The weaknesses of the novel are overborne, however, by its strengths. Its entertaining plot, engaging theme, and elements of farce and satire all go into making this a noteworthy novel by a promising writer. In assessing these strengths, we must recognize that because *Hurry on Down* was the work of a young novelist, it has the characteristic vitality of a young man's book. Wain wrote it in bursts of enthusiasm over a three-year span, during which time there were frequent pauses. The result is a novel whose focus changes several times. In spite of this fact, there is a freshness and verve in *Hurry on Down* that enhances its plot and an authenticity in its descriptions of the commercial world of the 1950s. With respect to its theme, Wain's novel is similar to his contemporaries' first novels.

The theme of the young man trying to escape the restriction imposed by class structure is one of the major subjects of the contemporary British novel. In an earlier period—say in 1900— these heroes would have been excluded from university educations, and their activities would have been channeled into working-class occupations. But the establishment of more universities and state scholarships allowed them to become educated. With an education, they were precluded from a working-class life but were still unacceptable, generally, to the Establishment. This theme was treated often in a satiric vein.

One of the earliest satires is found in Philip Larkin's first published novel, *Jill* (1946). Like Lumley, John Kemp is rejected and made uncomfortable because of his lower-class background. He feels himself an outsider, "caught" between the lower class of his background and the upper class to which his education has brought him. Because Christopher Warner, his cosmopolitan roommate at Oxford, repeatedly snubs him and takes advantage of him, Kemp retreats into a temporarily successful fantasy world built around an imaginary sister, Jill, and elegant stories of holidays in Wales and in an upper-class environment. When this world breaks apart, Kemp pursues an actual girl named Gillian. Eventually, when drunk, he has enough courage to kiss her.

Wain's treatment of Lumley is similar. Again, we see a young central character faced with discontinuity in his life, and we see Wain develop the tension between comedy and serious disillusionment so central to his fiction. Also, in both novels we find the theme of a young man's pursuit of a girl who has more breeding as well as beauty than himself. And like Larkin, Wain has a moral interest in the subject of class restrictions. He refers to this interest in "Along the Tightrope," his contribution to *Declaration,* when he writes:

When I wrote *Hurry on Down,* the main problem which had presented itself in my own existence was the young man's problem of how to adapt himself to "life," in the sense of an order external to himself, already there when he appeared on the scene, and not necessarily disposed to welcome him; the whole being complicated by the fact that in our civilization there is an unhealed split between the educational system and the assumptions that actually underlie daily life.[11]

Episodic, using the journey motif, *Hurry on Down* ties together locale and experience allowing Wain not only to lay bare a society but also to reveal his central character through his adventures. Lumley's character is established almost immediately with the description of his conflict with the landlady. We see him as the adaptable antihero who tries to control his own fate, as a jack of all trades, a skilled manipulator, an adept deceiver, an artist of disguises. Wain stresses Lumley's ingenuity rather than his mere struggle for survival; and, at the same time, he develops the individual personality of Lumley, emphasizing the man and his adventures. The fact that he makes his entry upon the stage in this particular fashion tells us something about him right away. The role that Lumley plays in the very first scene is one in which he will be cast throughout the story—that of a put-upon young man engaged in an attempt to cope with and outwit the workaday world.

This is not to say that Wain avoided digressing from the traditional in his characterization of Lumley. On the contrary, unlike the eighteenth-century picaro who is often hard-hearted, cruel, or selfish, Wain's central character is a well-intentioned drifter who compromises just enough to live comfortably. His standby and salvation is a strong sense of humor that enables him to make light of much distress and disaster. Lumley's character is revealed by playing it against the shifting setting of the picaresque world, together with his characteristic response to repeated assults on his fundamental decency and sympathy for others. The repetition comes through his willingness to start over again after each rebuke. He remains substantially the same throughout the novel. The many role changes—window cleaner, delivery driver, chauffeur, and the like—are examples of Wain's use of the picaresque tradition. Lumley's versatility and adaptability permit Wain to show his character under a variety of circumstances and in a multiplicity of situations.

Noteworthy, too, is that Lumley is no philosophical prober. He relates occurrences without offering much in the way of analysis. Since he lacks depth of personality, or memories, the reader sees his flat life. Through this device Wain estimates his vision of contemporary life: "an impoverished existence devoid of memory or meaning."[12] Hence, *Hurry on Down* is the adventurous story of a rogue's life, which through its episodic account of wanderings, adversity, and ingenious role-playing incorporates a satiric view of society.

The satire is developed through the characterization. Those who commit themselves to class—who judge others and define themselves by the class structure—are satirized throughout the novel. Surrounding the hero is a host of lightly sketched—"flat"—stock figures, all of whom play their predictable roles. These characters include the Proletarian Girl, the American, the landlady, the entrepreneur, the middle-class couple, and the artist. Wain's resources in characterization are limited primarily to caricature. The comedy functions to instruct and entertain. Beneath the horseplay and high spirits, Wain rhetorically manipulates our moral judgment so that we leave the novel sympathetic to the hero's point of view. In the tradition of Smollett and Dickens, Wain gives life to the grotesque by emphasizing details of his eccentric characters and by indicating his attitude toward them through the selection of specific bodily and facial characteristics. Although he does not say his characters are detestable, because of the language with which they are described Wain has made that inference inescapable.

One example should be enough to demonstrate Wain's technique—the introduction to the detestable writer, Edwin Froulish, a man to be neither admired nor trusted. Bohemian novelist Froulish claims to be a genius, but all of the images point to a charlatan leading a "profoundly ordinary existence."[13] His overcoat must have been taken from a scarecrow (p. 47). His figure is "ungainly, unkempt" (p. 32), with a "thick-set body" (p. 35) and a "twitching mask of dough with . . . pink deep-set eyes" (p. 37) and "lank" hair (p. 33). Moreover, he is eccentric, neurotic, a "sham artist" (p. 36) who engages in "sordid intellectual chatter" (p. 35) and lives off his wife, Betty, a "trousered tart" (p. 36). These details give us an idea, and a humorous one at that, of what sort of man is Froulish. We receive this idea, be it noted, from the author as seen through Lumley's eyes. Not only does he describe Froulish, but he comments humorously on what he is describing.

The impact of these images becomes more comical when we learn that Froulish dreams of being the subject of a monumental biography. He is distressed because he is unable to provide "material for quotable anecdotes" as did Pope, Southey, and Tennyson (p. 33). At the university he manages to get himself talked about by "carrying a grey parrot in a cage wherever he went, wearing a bowler hat indoors, standing motionless for hours on end in the exact centre of the quadrangle, and so forth" (p. 34). All of this physical description undercuts Froulish's role-playing and prepares us for one of the funniest and most memorable scenes in the novel.

This episode occurs when Froulish appears before the Stotwell Literary Society to read selections from his Work in Progress. The situation confirms all that we have been told about Froulish. He is, indeed, an eccentric, a monomaniac, a charlatan. He stands up, "his face a blind, twitching mask" (p. 56). He knocks a glass off the table in a gesture which "must surely have been intentional" (p. 56). He removes his collar and tie and throws them into the fire — "surely a contrived effect" (p. 57). He jerks his "left leg spasmodically" (p. 56).

By insisting on the grotesqueries and idiosyncracies of his characters, Wain provides a consistency in the environment of his picaresque world. Therefore, those in attendance who take Froulish seriously are satirized as well. Their grotesqueness is rooted either in some trait of personality or in some physical characteristic. In some figures, the two techniques are combined. The descriptions of June Veeber (who speaks in "bell-like" tones [p. 56]), Gunning-Forbes (who clears his throat "with a noise like a cavalry carbine being fired in a railway tunnel" [p. 56]), and Betty (who laughs with a "low neighing sound" [p. 62]) undercut their serious pretensions. The description of the members' arguments over Froulish's untitled work and its preamble is highly comical, too. At all events, these caricatured comic types are ideally suited as foils for Wain's hero to use in his discovery of the world of folly and fraud.

What is more, Wain varies his caricature from personality to personality. Each time the device is employed, it enlarges our notions of the *kinds* of absurdities and exaggeration present within the picaro's world. There is, for instance, Arthur Blearney's gang of effeminate highbrows and factitious sophisticates. As Lumley approaches a party, their supposed sophistication is undercut when Lumley notices how much like the cries of anguish are the noises of the people assembled to have a good time:

Mr. Blearney's voice, grating on as he told one of his stories, might have been the endless mumbling delirium of a man in great pain. The roars of laughter which punctuated it, reaching him muffled through two closed doors, sounded like the bellowing of a herd of cattle driven towards the slaughter-house. And one woman shrieked at intervals as if she were being disembowelled. (p. 102)

Here again, Wain exaggerates for comic effect: surely Blearney is not really in pain, and obviously the anonymous woman is not being disemboweled. Nor is there literally a herd of cattle behind the closed doors; that is the author's amusing way of putting it, the metaphor being that of a herd of cattle being slaughtered. It is the storyteller's manner, and we enjoy it.

The physical description of the guests confirms the impression created by their voices. Upon entering the house, Lumley finds that "they looked studiedly theatrical instead of harmlessly eccentric, and gave no impression, *en masse,* of intelligence or sensitivity" (p. 103). When he is introduced as "Harry Lumpy" (p. 104), "the succession of names flooded over his mind like dirty water" (p. 104). Notice how Wain uses descriptive adjectives and extended commentary to poke fun at the supposed sophisticate in the following scene:

The group seemed to be dominated . . . by a thick-set, middle-aged man in a loud check suit, who had the biggest face Charles had ever seen. Its total area was big, and all its features were big. Huge eyebrows arched over protruding eyes. His mouth seemed immense even when, as now, he happened to have it closed for the moment. His nose was both long and fantastically bulbous, with nostrils like volcanic craters, from which black hairs peered. Hairs of about the same length covered the backs of his hands. (p. 103)

Without a doubt, these fictional creations remind us of Dickens's rogues whose physical deformities are intended to suggest the corruption of their souls. Although undercutting characterizations in themselves might seem to be merely the petulant commentary of a particularly uncharitable young writer, they are meant to be believed. Therefore, the exaggeratedly humorous statements involved in these characterizations serve an underlying purpose: the reader realizes all along that the author means these observations as serious moral commentary.

The indirect presence of the storyteller is very important to the humor not only of these scenes, but in most of what follows in the novel. It is the active role of this authorial impresario telling the story to us that accounts for the distance between the reader and the events of the novel. The conscious presence of the performing storyteller, with his exaggerations, his jokes, and his philosophizing, creates the distance and detachment needed to make us view Lumley's exploits in the proper way. While we are able to see things as Lumley sees them—and Lumley is a very acute and discerning observer—we also view Lumley as he sees and thinks from the author's vantage point. Because the storyteller is obviously for the most part good-humored and rather fond of Lumley, we are never allowed to take events so seriously that they become pathetic or tragic. In later novels, this attitude will change as Wain's tragic vision deepens.

Any discussion of comic technique in *Hurry on Down* brings us inevitably to the novel's resolution. Ordinarily, we do not like to encounter "perfect" endings to our novels; nevertheless, we are not put off by the unrealistic ending to this novel because we know from the beginning that we are reading a comic novel which depends upon unrealistic exaggeration of various kinds. Elgin W. Mellown was correct when he called the novel "a pastiche: Walter Mitty's desire expressed through the actions of the Three Stooges—wish fulfillment carried out through outrageous actions and uncharacteristic behavior."[14] We feel secure in the rightness of the ending as a conclusion to all of the comic wrongness that has gone on before. The happy ending is not contrived; it comes about naturally.

What we remember best are those comic moments. Lumley is less an angry young man than a funny, bumbling, confused individual for whom a joke makes life more bearable. There are, of course, other ways to react to an unjust world. One can flail at it, as does Jimmy Porter. One can escape from it, as Edgar Banks will try to do in Wain's next novel. Or one can try to adapt to it. Like Jim Dixon's rebellion against the affectation of academia, Lumley's opposition to middle-class values ends with an adjustment to the society and with a partial acceptance of its values. By remaining "in" the system, he can at least try to effect change. Porter, on the outside, can do little more than rage.

As we have seen, *Hurry on Down* is an exercise in the picaresque, in which the hero bumps through various sectors of the picaresque world. Each incident reveals Lumley's point of view by presenting him with situations in which he is unable either to adjust or to communicate. This device of stringing anecdotes upon a narrative thread allows the narrator to introduce a large number of vivid character portraits. Through Lumley, the narrator becomes an observer of humanity and its foibles.

Although *Hurry on Down* cannot be read today with anything like the enthusiasm with which many readers initially received it, the undimmed sparkle and vitality of the humor indicate what delighted audiences then. Writing of it in 1978, Wain placed it fairly accurately: *Hurry on Down* was a "youthful firework display [with] inexperience stamped on every page," but it nevertheless "managed to hit a mood that a lot of people were dimly conscious of feeling."[15]

It is indeed a young man's book, immaturely imagined, and, as several critics complained, often just verging on the superficial, but it was addressed to the youth of its day, and its appeal was immediate. Its popularity derived not only from its youthfulness but from its spirit of non-conformity and adventure. It was one of the first novels to tackle with any degree of freshness the problems confronting youth in post-war Britain, and through Wain's hero there sounded clearly that note of disillusionment that was to become dominant in the literature of the so-called Angry Young Men.

In Wain's next novel, however, we find that disillusionment turns into despair, the picaresque becomes a quest, and the picaro becomes a suicidal protagonist—all of which gives the novel a mock-melodramatic dimension.

II   Living in the Present

Published in 1955 and reissued in 1960, *Living in the Present* is another study of a character who seeks escape from his social past. However, while Lumley's goal is classlessness, Edgar Banks's goal is death. Whereas Lumley is concerned with how to live, Banks is concerned with how to die. Although it is doubtful that anyone knows finally how to take it, *Living in the Present* gives the impression of a deeply personal work.

Obviously drawing upon the picaresque tradition once again, Wain centers the plot on Edgar Banks, a twenty-nine-year-old schoolteacher who intends to kill himself and thereby escape from the boredom and pointlessness of human life. Through a series of flashbacks, we see the number of failures that have caused him to lose any desire to live. To leave the world a little better, he also plots to kill the most loathsome and immoral creature he knows. He selects for his victim Rollo Philipson-Smith, a snide, class-conscious Neo-Fascist who is involved in a mysterious, unexplained "Movement." However, at every crucial moment, when he is about to kill Philipson-Smith, something intervenes. One time Banks is about to push him over a cliff when he sees a child climbing a dangerous tree. His yelling out to save the child also saves Philipson-Smith from certain death. Another time Banks is unable to crash the car in which he is driving his victim.

Still intent on his plan, Banks chases Philipson-Smith and his foolish Scots follower, McWhirtner, from London to Switzerland and Italy. Along the way he encounters Mr. and Mrs. Crabshaw and their children. He also meets Mirabelle, an American journalist who goes to bed with him but fails to rid him of his twin obsessions with murder and suicide. Only Catharine, the fiancée of Tom Straw and an old friend of Banks, is able to achieve this.

Banks falls in love with Catharine, marries her, and for the first time in his life experiences happiness. With this newfound joy comes a release from his suicidal complex. After he regains his hold on life, Banks is amazed that he ever planned to kill himself: "the bad yesterdays and the wonderful to-morrows. It was over. He was tired of living in the present."[16] He even returns to work for Simms, the schoolmaster who was at least partly responsible for Banks's deathwish in the first place. Having finally affirmed life, Banks has the hope of the future to sustain him in the present. Through Tom and Catharine, Banks has found his own meaning for goodness, honesty, and love—qualities of sufficient worth to justify living in the future.

Inevitably, the critics of *Living in the Present* hastened to compare it to *Hurry on Down*, and most of them found it to lack a certainty of purpose. A fundamental weakness of the novel is that the pervading atmosphere of death is far in excess of the situation, and the despair is insufficiently motivated. Unlike his first novel, this work is a flawed, only an intermittently funny novel of misfired opportunities and isolated pieces of information. A great deal of what is apparently offered as comedy is not funny enough to be that. Although Wain had intended it as a joke at the expense of fashionable despair and nihilism, reviewers attacked it as both nihilistic and despairing. Consequently, the book was neither an artistic nor a financial success and fully deserves Wain's verdict: "The less said about this book, . . . the better."[17]

The case against the book was put most forcibly by Wain himself. In the 1960 preface to the American edition, he said that the plot was too mechanical and that he followed it too rigidly. He tried to manipulate an artificial quest theme, built into a framework of foreign travel. The result is that the novel begins with a certain amount of vitality, runs into a marsh halfway through, and does not regain pace until the end. *Hurry on Down*, by contrast, has a fast-moving plot from beginning to end. The reader wants to read on. To develop the plot of *Living in the Present*, Wain drew from Graham Greene, A. Conan Doyle, and the serialized cliff-hanger to complicate a simple story line. Thus we find such stock elements as unexplained references to the mysterious "Movement" and shadowy figures and fantastic scenes which compete with rather than complement the main story. While entertaining in themselves, these techniques do not cohere to a central purpose.

A further problem in this novel is inherent in its ambiguous tone. *Hurry on Down* is unmistakably farcical with serious undertones. Lumley's experiences at Blearney's party or at the Literary Society are clearly meant to be comic, and there is no doubt that Wain is intentionally ridiculing the minor characters. But in *Living in the Present*, the wordplay and verbal jokes are unclear. It is difficult to know when the author is being funny and when he is being serious.

This inconsistency extends also to the characterization. It is difficult to know whether or not to take Banks seriously. Again written about from the third-person, omniscient point of view, the hero and his problems never convince us of their reality. At times, his encounters abroad with Mrs. Crabshaw as she "protects" her family, for example, are funny. His travels with the children, his rendezvous with the American reporter Mirabelle, and his journey across Switzerland all offer genuinely amusing moments in the novel. But his four murder attempts are ludicrous, and we wonder if Wain is attempting, though unsuccessfully, to provide the same mixture of farce and seriousness we see in Lumley. Because Banks's character is ill-defined, and because Wain employs a rough-and-ready attempt to mix the grotesque with the somber, the normal is undermined and made unbelievable. Therefore, Banks's return to respectability at the end is unconvincing, too. "After being treated to a farcical nihilism it is difficult to accept serious respectability with a straight face."[18]

Along with Banks's ambiguous character stand Wain's minor characters, who, with one exception, seldom convince us of their reality. Instead, they move about like two-dimensional puppets. Philipson-Smith, for instance, is a stock figure often found in fiction, drama, and movies. There is nothing new about him. Only in Catharine's characterization does Wain come close to his potential talent for realistic portrayal. She is presented as a contrasting picture of serious health: "This girl was a real person, living consciously and steadily, moving towards definite objects" (p. 175). She is the goal of respectability toward which the hero eventually strives; her stability—the very absence of flaws in her makeup—serves to contrast her with the grotesque and unstable values of the picaresque world.

One further reason for the novel's weakness is that the moral problems carry little weight. At the center of the novel is a hinted moral concern: " 'I have been reminded of a responsibility towards life,' " Banks writes. " 'Formerly aware of the respon-

sibility of hatred. Now of the responsibility of goodwill' "
(p. 185). Underlining this, he goes on immediately: ' "Dislike of
Philipson-Smith (embodies evil) balanced by liking for Tom
Straw (embodies good). Responsibility extending both ways' "
(p. 185). But Wain does little with this theme, and, because of the
ambiguity of tone and character, it falls flat. We cannot tell if
Wain approves or disapproves of his characters. Because of this
uncertainty, the moral seriousness we saw in *Hurry on Down* is
not discernible in this novel.

All of which brings us to the most serious defect of all: the
whole story is confusing because of what seems to be a
fundamental indecision in Wain's mind. For about the first half of
the book, the theme is the familiar one of the outsider seeking
escape from an unbearable life, but the remainder of the novel
never satisfies this. A confusion of motives and insufficient
objectivity blurs Wain's vision, and his failure fully to grasp the
significance of his subject matter makes it difficult for him to
clearly develop his theme.

This is not to imply that the novel is without its strengths.
Although the book's many ambiguities were an easy target for
the hostile critic, those predisposed to listen to the testament of
youth saw in it the work of a writer of promise. Wain's accurate
social documentation—his depiction of everyday, realistic details
of life to which we can all relate—is one of his most praised skills.
And some of the comic scenes are memorable for their
exaggeration. But perhaps G. S. Fraser's essay contains the best
account of its positive merits:

A novel of his which never, I think, got the praise that was its due was
his second, *Living in the Present*, which, under the guise of a satirical
and farcical melodrama, is a very gripping and uncomfortable study in
the pathology of rage. . . . The sense running through [it] of the
author's driving energy, lacerated amusement, and scornful rage
compensates for implausibilities and two-dimensional (all black and
white, or black and then white) characters. But even through parody
and exaggeration, Wain, like Amis, is one of the few living novelists who
give us a sense of actual contemporary life.[19]

Banks's quest, however inconsequential and, at times absurd,
epitomized that of the rising generation, and his gesture of
revolt, however indefinite, awoke many echoes. In his cynicism,
world-weariness, and regret for lost joys, Banks is the archetypal

hero of the 1950s, for Wain, like John Osborne in *Look Back in Anger*, gives expression to a generation's mood of discontent and rebellion.

The similarities between *Hurry on Down* and *Living in the Present* are readily perceived. In both novels we find a straightforward linear chronology unfolded through the agency of the omniscient third-person narrator. As the protagonists, Charles Lumley and Edgar Banks rebel against the picaresque world, but by the end accept the kind of class and social role demanded by their time, place, and training. They also learn that genuine value is purely personal. And most important to Wain's thematic concerns, both characters are outsiders uncertain about the necessity and desirability of becoming insiders.

There are, however, a couple of major differences between these books. One is a difference in point of view, in underlying assumptions, that ultimately amounts to a difference in kind. Whatever we may think of the horseplay, *Hurry on Down* gives us a truly comic resolution: it leaves us rejoicing over Lumley's moral triumph. On the other hand, for what little laughter it provokes—and much of that is ambiguous—*Living in the Present* approaches tragedy as it brings Banks to the verge of despair. The comic tone in *Hurry on Down* is both obvious and consistent. Because the tone in *Living in the Present* is neither obvious nor consistent, Banks's experience becomes pathetic and melodramatic, and we are unprepared for the final turnabout in his fortunes at the end. What is more, the details in the second novel suggest a certain coarseness on the part of author and hero. Because it is told from the hero's point of view, we can escape neither his despair nor the feeling that Banks's point of view is attributable to Wain.

The second difference is that of the two heroes, Banks is the duller, less adequately developed character. Many critics viewed him as a failure of invention. And because he is a disappointing bore, there is little fun in this novel. These differences help to account for its unkind reception by critics. In the minds of many reviewers, Wain was a one-novel writer whose early success was due more to luck than to talent.[20]

In his next novel, however, Wain puts to rest many of the skeptics with a more mature, more controlled study in which seriousness is balanced by humor and derision is tempered by patience and affection.

III   The Contenders

As the title suggests, Wain's next novel concerns the corrupting nature of material ambition and rivalry and the value of work. It is also, Wain says, an explanation of metropolitan versus provincial virtues: " 'being in touch' versus 'sturdy independence.' "[21] As expected, Wain chooses the provinces against the emptiness of the city. *The Contenders* is a much less ambiguous, much more complex performance than *Living in the Present*.

The Contenders is the story of three provincial youths who go separate ways in the world in their attempt to find what they value in life. In place of the episodic plot, Wain uses a simple and rapidly moving story which gains momentum from a single conflict between two friends and an observer. Robert Lamb, the artist, is talented, moody, explosive, egotistical, and impulsive. He goes to London, where he pursues his fortune as an artist. Ned Roper, the businessman, is neat, self-controlled, determined, calm, organized, and methodical. He becomes an industrialist. Joe Shaw, their friend, is an easygoing, noncompetitive newspaperman. As the narrator, he looks on from the sidelines, reports the events, and reluctantly serves as a buffer between the two competitors who are locked in a struggle for success.

Shaw first met Lamb and Roper when all three of them were enrolled in a boys' school near London. Since their childhood, Lamb and Roper had been taught that life is competitive. The effects of this training become obvious when they leave school. Roper takes over the family's pottery firm, brings it out of its depression slump of the 1930s, and becomes a financial success. Lamb, on the other hand, quickly leaves the pottery-designing job Ned had offered him and heads for London to live the life of the Bohemian. He is promoted eventually as a brilliant young painter whose works are commanding fantastic prices. During this time, Shaw heals their bitter quarrels and preserves their friendship.

Not long after his success, Lamb meets and marries a popular fashion model, Myra Chetwynd, only to lose her several years later to the still more successful Roper. Then Lamb takes up with a young Italian girl named Pepina, but he deserts her to chase after Ned and Myra, who have since gone to Paris on their honeymoon. In a comic reversal, Shaw finally finds Pepina, rescues her from a job in a London café, and, presumably, marries her. Happy to be through at last with his unwilling participation in an unending contest, Shaw has a final mental vision of "Ned and Robert running down the Champs-Elysées passing Myra's head back and forth like a football."[22] Once again his own man, Joe returns to London with Pepina. The contenders have become so intent on outdoing one another that the prizes for which they contend have faded into insignificance.

After the appearance of *The Contenders,* Wain waited anxiously to see what critics would say. He was not disappointed, for most reviewers were enthusiastic. Admirers of Wain were relieved to find that the novel was both a technical and a thematic advance over his earlier work. James Gindin said it was "a more searching examination of [contemporary] society."[23] Milton Crane called it a "skillfully wrought satirical novel" in which Wain's forte is the "big comic scene, imagined and executed in virtually dramatic terms."[24] To Elgin W. Mellown, *The Contenders* was another wish-fulfillment novel with a sharper point of view and a unity of theme and form.[25] Geoffrey Nicholson was pleasantly surprised by Wain's "extremely vigorous" writing and by his "intelligent and sympathetic" attitude.[26] Roger Pippett said that the novel defied classification: it is a novel of "character, a picaresque extravaganza, a social satire, a modern morality, . . . [and] a cautionary tale."[27] And William Van O'Connor said that with this novel Wain's "down-to-earth morality"[28] becomes evident. It is what Wain has been searching for all along.

Unlike the heroes of Wain's first two novels, Joe Shaw successfully rejects dominant patterns of contemporary society in favor of an older, more local tradition. Shaw is seen at his best when he stays with what he knows and can handle, when he avoids the pretense implicit in the cosmopolitan. Also, in both technique and theme, *The Contenders* is more complex and more sophisticated than either *Hurry on Down* or *Living in the Present.* Although it contains elements of farce and several humorous episodes, it is a work of seriousness. What makes it the best of Wain's three novels is the combination of a sharper point of view, a vivid satiric characterization, a unity of theme and form, and a witty narrative style.

If we contrast *The Contenders* with the earlier novels, several marked differences in technique become apparent. Once again,

Wain limits the point of view to one central figure. But unlike his first two novels, both of which were written from third-person omniscience, Wain chose the first-person narration for *The Contenders*. Joe Shaw relates the events as they happen from his vantage point of several years after their occurrence. There is, therefore, an intimacy established between narrator and reader which does not exist in *Hurry on Down* and *Living in the Present*. By the time he is telling the story, Shaw is successful and is looking back to the period when he still had a choice about his future. Only twice in the novel are we reminded that Shaw is speaking of events that occurred several years before. He seems to be telling the story as it happens most of the time. Because of his position, our evaluation of characters depends almost entirely upon Shaw's descriptions of and reactions to them. Although Wain still intrudes indirectly to order the events and to set up the scenes, our moral concern is affected primarily by what Shaw tells us.

Because of the limitations imposed by the first-person narration, almost no use is made of subplot in *The Contenders*. That is, in the space of the novel, there is little room for Shaw to tell other stories; because he is concerned with relating the conflicts between his two friends, he is seldom interested in reporting affairs that do not directly affect him. Almost all of Shaw's energies—until near the end of the novel—revolve around his relationship with Lamb and Roper. There are only a few places in the novel that show him as much concerned about other people. The point of view is, therefore, a technical advance for Wain.

Characterization is another technical advance for Wain. In the first place the portraits of the characters are much fuller in this novel. In *Hurry on Down* and *Living in the Present* little attention is given to any part of a character's past which is not immediately relevant to the present action. But in *The Contenders*, Wain shows a great deal of concern for past history and provides what amounts to small biographies of Roper, Lamb, and Shaw. However, this concern with character detail is not immediately apparent. At first, the reader thinks the novel is about Lamb and Roper as contenders, with Shaw as merely the mouthpiece for the story. Its opening states: "This is the story of two men, Robert Lamb and Ned Roper" (p. 1). Soon we realize that although both men are at the center of the novel, it is Shaw recording and evaluating what happens that makes the subject of the novel. So the book is in a great sense Shaw's story.

For the realization of this story, Wain adopted a single yet effective technique. With the example of F. Scott Fitzgerald's *The Great Gatsby* before him, he abandoned the omniscient viewpoint of his previous novels to present Roper's and Lamb's stories through the eyes of a fictional narrator at once implicated in and detached from the main action. Like Nick Carraway of Fitzgerald's novel, Shaw adopts a moral stance which modifies our judgment of what he describes and whose sensibility and intelligence mediate between the action and the reader. Also like Carraway, Shaw develops while he observes. Through his association with Roper and Lamb, the acting characters, Shaw as the narrating character learns about himself as well as his friends.

Because the events and the characters are interpreted and judged through Shaw's mind, Wain quickly establishes his character—his interests, his morality, his prejudices. As an advocate of traditional values, Shaw serves as the voice of moderation, the moral consciousness which perceives the absurdities in others' lives yet fails to steer them away from the destructive course they are on. He ridicules complete devotion to Art and reverence for material success. He attacks the spirit of competition motivating both of his friends. This, he observes, is a spirit instilled by parents, teachers, all of society. Simple and noncompetitive, Shaw resists adherence to commercial and middle-class values.

Another major theme in this novel is the value of localism. Shaw has never really left the pottery town in which he grew up. He has not been corrupted by the cosmopolitan influence of London. He is aware of London's many limitations, but fond of it. Shaw's—and hence, Wain's—down-to-earth morality becomes evident when he observes that Roper's artistic abilities are attributable to his years in the provinces:

The only reason England has any intellectual and artistic life at all is because men like Robert aren't reared in London. They take their originality with them, and London consumes it all and gives them nothing back. It's because the provinces accept dreariness that London can boast of its brilliance. (p. 49)

At one point, Lamb even requires a return to his provincial origins to find himself and regain his talent. Thus Shaw's basically sound, humane, provincial point of view is contrasted to Roper and Lamb's obsession with worldly success and ultimately with inhuman competition.

As in his first two novels, Wain's sympathies are once again with the underdog; however, this doesn't keep Wain from poking fun at Shaw, too. Fat, easygoing, and noncompetitive, Shaw goes out of his way to picture himself as anything but the heroic type. When war seems uncertain, Lamb and Roper sign up early to secure the kind of jobs they want. As for Shaw, "It was all too obvious," he says, "that I would stay quietly at home until I was actually *made* to join up. I'm the stuff of which the rank and file of every British army is made" (p. 98).

Many of the most amusing passages are remarks Shaw makes as asides to us in the course of the narrative. When he takes the half-starved Lamb to a café one day shortly after the war, he explains that this was a time when in England "you had to go down on your knees for a ham sandwich, and for a hot meal you had practically to sign an undertaking that the landlord could be named as your sole legatee, requisition your house and garden, sleep with your wife and/or sister and wipe his boots on your waistcoat" (p. 108). On another occasion, as Roper and Shaw approach the mansion Lamb has acquired in his quick rise from starvation to opulence, Shaw extends a silent welcome: "Welcome to Liberality Hall. Come and join the brilliant throng of thronging brilliance. I wondered why I had not had the sense to stay at home, but Ned was already thronging up the garden path, so I thronged after him and we thronged in" (p. 122).

Moreover, in characteristic fashion, Wain allows his narrative point of view to provide the vehicle for his satiric attacks. Wherever Shaw travels, whatever he does, Wain chooses targets for satire. Nothing misses: crockery designs, national mores, Philistinism, guests of a celebrity, Bohemian life, art patron, dining-car steward—all become objects of satire through Shaw's presence, through Shaw's experience.

Finally, as in *Hurry on Down,* Wain turns to caricature to poke fun at some of the minor characters as well. Bloater, one of Shaw's schoolmasters, is able and intelligent. However, Shaw comments: "I suppose the reason why he didn't get an academic job was just because nobody could stand his guts" (p. 16). Randall, another teacher, is described as being "a middle-aged man with spindly legs and a beer-drinker's paunch" (p. 86). Celia, Lamb's first mistress, "had a pair of ear-rings on that looked as if they were made of wood, and she was carrying a big leather bag which seemed to be full of potatoes" (p. 52). Stocker, whose lecherous tendencies showed up while he was still a schoolboy, keeps a careful mental record of a number of women he has had, although he does not remember names or places and cannot even remember what they looked like sometimes (p. 4). Shaw also indulges in comic exaggeration. At the dinner table, Lamb "gorged like a man driven insane by hunger" (p. 108); a teacher's "eyes were as watery as a bloodhound's and you could light a stove with his breath" (p. 86).

We see, therefore, that in *The Contenders* Wain has subdued the picaresque element to a more complex purpose. Point of view, satiric characterization, theme and form, and a witty narrative style contribute to a unified study into the corrupting nature of material ambition and the benefits of provincial over metropolitan values. Noteworthy, too, is that the comedy is better integrated with the rest of the book.

In spite of these advances, however, there is yet little depth to his characters. As Max Cosman wrote: "Basically [Wain] is an inquisitor of belief and an irrepressible censor of behavior. But at the same time he is a writer fallible in his craft, still apt to contrive when he should perceive, and to verbalize when he should be subtle."[29] This problem will persist in his next novel, in which Wain subdues the picaresque element to examine twentieth-century morals in marriage.

IV A Travelling Woman

In his fourth novel, Wain borrows in part from Restoration comedy to write about the sterility and the lack of meaning in contemporary marriage. As in his first three novels, Wain's central characters find they need to reassess their own moral values to find a code by which to live. Although they chase some image of romantic fulfillment which they think is unique, each situation fits into the same sordid design of people trying to avoid the boredom of fidelity.[30] Love played a secondary role in his earlier works, but in this novel the author is almost exclusively concerned with sexual relationships. The anguish of adultery is a central concern in A *Travelling Woman.*

Although Wain employs the third-person omniscient point of view, the omniscience covers only one character at a time. The novel represents a new departure for Wain, because he leaves behind the pattern of the first three novels to focus, in part, on a heroine. The entertainment is made of two sets of complications involving eight characters: George Links and his wife, Janet; Edward Cowley, his wife, Ruth, and son, Teddy; Evan Bone and his wife, Barbara; and Fredric Captax.

Events move quickly. Because George Links, a young lawyer, is plagued by chronic boredom with life, Janet Links, his wife, suggests that he go to a psychiatrist. He likes this suggestion because it will afford him the opportunity to make overnight visits to London, where he engages in an adulterous affair with Ruth Cowley. Ironically, Ruth is married to a man who has lost his religious faith after writing a best-seller called *The Discovery of Faith.* Either he is blind to the truth about his wife or he prefers not to know.

In the meantime, Janet learns about her husband's romance and has an affair of her own with Fredric Captax, a bogus analyst who takes advantage of George's excursions and gets a room for him at the Cowleys'.

To complicate the story even further, friends of Captax—Evan and Barbara Bone—appear on the scene. Barbara is attracted to George, but he is not attracted to her. Eventually, after Janet has broken off with Captax, George wants to reconcile with Janet; however, even though she has left Captax, she refuses. George realizes too late that to find contentment, he should have been true to his wife. He misses her gentleness and concern. Thus, he learns that a single and permanent relationship is of utmost importance for true happiness. Cowley also realizes that he must remain loyal to his best seller and its implications.[31] The human being is too limited, personally and intellectually, to handle the freedom that his powers of logical analysis suggest. Man is too feeble to do without his commitments.[32] It is a conclusion that foreshadows the theme of much of Wain's subsequent fiction.

For a number of reasons the critical reception to A *Travelling Woman* was not enthusiastic. Reviewers pointed out difficulties with Wain's haphazard style, unconvincing characterization, and

thematic ambiguities. George Bluestone felt that the basic
weakness lay in the novel's remarkably inconclusive ending,
offering further evidence that "Wain has nothing fundamental to
quarrel with."[33] William Van O'Connor attributed the failure of
A Travelling Woman to Wain's confused attitude, his "wanting to
be a wit and needing to be a moralist."[34] Elgin W. Mellown
objected to Wain's attitude toward George Links, whom he finds
to be dull and inadequate.[35]

In spite of these criticisms, A Travelling Woman is a step
forward insofar as Wain is able to stay within the convention of
Restoration comedy he sets up. In the manner of Wycherley,
Congreve, and others, the sexual relations in this novel are
entirely dominated by a set of conventions for the amusement
they afford. The first convention is that constancy, especially in
marriage, is a bore, and love only thrives on variety. Wain
unambiguously attributes this attitude to Links. He exhibits
Fredric Captax in an identical vein. For these two characters as
well as for Ruth Cowley, Barbara Bone, and Janet Links, appetite
needs perpetually fresh stimulus.

Second, again borrowing from Restoration comedy, sentiments
such as these are not offered for straightforward acceptance;
instead, they are attributed to characters plainly marked as
foolish or absurd (Captax, for example, is a "pyknic type, with a
potato-face and domed forehead" [p. 6]) or, more frequently, as
trivial, and Wain can, therefore, dissociate himself. The characters with some life in them have nothing to fall back on—nothing,
that is, except the conventional, and conventionally limited,
pleasures of sex. The conventions of sexual pursuit, and so on, are
an attempt to make life interesting.

Another parallel to the drama in A Travelling Woman is
apparent when we turn from an analysis of character to an
examination of the staging of the novel. The chief structural
device is the progression from one self-contained scene to
another. Each chapter is a separate, dramatically rendered
scene, composed of action and dialogue, and usually set off in the
action by the entrance or exit of one or more characters. Wain
uses the standard features of the love-intrigue plot to motivate
the story; in this case the operative questions are: Who will get
the man? Who will get the woman? The whole of the book is the
development of all the various love relationships. Although there
is nothing startling about a writer's moving his story forward in a

series of scenes, Wain's rather short scenes with an emphasis on dialogue are a dominant mark of his structure and influence the totality of the novel. The action moves at a fast clip and is limited to the Linkses' living room, Captax's home, the saloon bar, the Cowleys' kitchen and attic, and the train station. The characters are seen isolated or in small groups as they might be on a sparsely furnished stage. Even Wain's scenic descriptions suggest the theater: "the countryside seemed a stage set, gay and warmly lit" (p. 8). There is also a minimum of narration; the novel is primarily a series of conversations in which Wain dramatizes thoughts.

Wain departs from this scenic principle, however, with an experimental method that becomes increasingly important in his later novels. Almost every chapter-scene is presented from the point of view of one of the participating characters—going into the unspoken reactions of one of the characters. For example, in one of the scenes involving George, Edward, and Ruth alone, Wain gives, in brief notations, George's reactions, his unexpressed thoughts, bewilderments, and emotions. Wain's use of this technique gives a slant to each scene, a position from which to see the action.

The most important technique within the scene is Wain's handling of dialogue. The operative principle that stands out in the dialogue of *A Travelling Woman* is a question-and-answer technique. In this, two characters, usually, attempt to analyze or simply understand the details of the action and to comprehend each other's motives or the motives of some absent character. Often the results are comic. The scene between Janet and Fred, in which Fred pretends to be George's psychiatrist, is an excellent example of the humorous possibilities. An example of the continual attempt on the part of the characters to get at each other's motives can be found in the saloon bar scenes among George, Fred, and the Bones couple. The effect of this technique throughout the novel is to increase the comedy and, more important, to emphasize repeatedly the failures in communication between individuals.

In spite of the Restoration-comedy conventions and the entertaining, fast-paced scenes, however, nothing fresh and penetrating is said about sex and sexual relations. As William Van O'Connor correctly assessed, Wain does not maintain the conventions to the end, nor does he develop the theme that they seem to promise. The conventions ask that "the sex game be seen in all its comic absurdity."[36] The novel is comic at the start, but at the end the action is resolved suddenly in a wholly realistic way. This lack of consistency blurs the novel's focus and weakens its impact upon the reader. This weakness prompted John Coleman to label *A Travelling Woman* "a confusion of high comedy and dangling motivations."[37] To Robert Gutwillig, the novel lacked "imaginative pressure [and was] clumsily plotted, carelessly written and peopled with ciphers."[38] As in his first three novels, Wain seems to have trouble with getting far below personal surfaces.

V   *Conclusion*

What *Hurry on Down, Living in the Present, The Contenders,* and *A Travelling Woman* share is a young hero who tries to separate himself from a world which he believes does not understand him and which strangles every attempt at individuality. It is a world with considerable unpleasantness in it, and there is a great deal about the hero's life that involves boredom, frustration, and violence. In each instance, the attempted breakaway ends in compromise despite the semblance of freedom.

Second, all four novels suggest that Wain's major strength as a novelist lies in character delineation. The principal techniques he uses are fairly simple: caricature through exaggerated description; a careful attention to dialogue, point of view, and action; and generalized psychological attributes—boredom, frustration, despair. Except for Joe Shaw, there is very little examination of motive beyond the obvious. The comic tone is most obvious in Wain's descriptions of the characters in *Hurry on Down.* The novel's attitude helps to keep Lumley's experiences from being too pathetic, holds the injustice of his world at a distance; and the decrease in comic touches of this sort in *The Contenders* heightens and solemnizes Wain's message.

Simplicity in exaggeration and concern with motive brings us to a major criticism of Wain's early comic novels: there is little suspense because the characters seem peculiarly unmotivated, put through their paces in a clever, mechanical way. Part of this problem is inherent in the plotting. It is the formless succession of events typical of the picaresque novel in which the *picaro,* or rogue, comments during his travels upon the vices of all levels of society. What does hold the reader's interest is the succeeding exposures of hypocrisy and various other twentieth century "evils" his figures perceive.

But the lack of suspense is related also to the psychological reality of the characters, which we find is of less consequence than the social message which the lives of the characters suggest. Sometimes Wain's attempt to mix "the grotesquely comic with the sombre or even tragic"[39] blurs the themes.

Although his characters' honesty, clever irony, and satire signify a disgust with contemporary England, these novels suggest that Wain has not found the artistic focus for an intense personal vision of the world. While Wain has not completely developed the structural techniques and themes which are to dominate his later novels, the matters are there in embryo. *Living in the Present* and *A Travelling Woman* anticipate his later work by dealing, however unsatisfactorily, with some subjects of central concern to him. The majority of his novels show an isolated protagonist painfully aware of his isolation. Although a much greater proportion of his later work connects isolation and loneliness with love or its absence, we can see operating here the same assumptions about human relationships, namely their fragility and ephemerality, which occupy so much of his attention in the late fiction. At the same time, early Wain is offering the sense that relationships, however inadequate, are more satisfying than isolation. In spite of certain weaknesses, therefore, these early novels are an impressive trial that foreshadows later achievements.

Wain's next novel testifies to his deepening personal vision and to his growth as an artist. He gives up the slapstick and sight gags which, although often hilarious, submerge the serious moral concern and, on occasion, diminish the credibility of his early novels. Like Lumley, Banks, Shaw, and Links, the writer's next protagonist rejects a world; unlike them, he finds his inner and outer freedom without compromising himself.

CHAPTER 3

The Odyssey of Youth

About his aims as a novelist, Wain wrote:

Naturally I know some areas of life better than others, but one of my aims is to go on extending these areas and adding new ones. . . . This constant alertness, the incessant struggle to bring fresh territory within one's imaginative range, seems to me also the highest form of experimentation.[1]

IN *Strike the Father Dead* (1962), Wain further extends himself with a work more penetrating than anything he has written before. Not only is it, as one critic said, a "deeply pondered novel,"[2] but it is also a culmination of the promises inherent in Wain's earlier novels. Ostensibly another example of the familiar story of initiation, in which a sensitive young man is confronted by external reality, *Strike the Father Dead* contains subtleties and ironies which set it apart. Plot, theme, character, and setting are integrated to tell the story of a son who breaks parental ties, thereby freeing himself to make his own way in life as a jazz pianist. Pointing to the foibles of his fellow man and probing the motives of an indignant parent, Wain's wit and sarcastic humour lighten at times the heavy tones of this study of the nonconformist's right to assert his nonconformity.

I Plot

The plot of the novel is arranged in an elaborate seven-part time scheme: Parts One and Six occur sometime late in 1957 or early in 1958; Part Two takes place while the hero is in the immediate prewar years; and the other divisions follow chronologically up to the last, which is set in 1958. The scene moves from between a provincial university town and the darker, black-market-and-jazz side of London, with a side trip to Paris.[3]

Wain narrates the story from the points of view of four characters. The central figure, Jeremy Coleman, revolts against his father and the academic environment in search of self-expression as a jazz pianist. Alfred Coleman, Jeremy's father and professor of classics, is an atheist devoted to duty and hard work. Eleanor, Alfred's sister and foster mother to Jeremy, is devoted to Jeremy and finds comfort in innocent religiosity. Percy Brett, a black American jazz musician, offers Jeremy his first real parental leadership. The hero's development is reminiscent of Samuel Butler's *The Way of All Flesh*. Like Ernest Pontifex, Jeremy escapes from under an oppressive existence; he has a passion for music, and once he has the opportunity to develop, his shrinking personality changes. First we see Jeremy as Alfred and Eleanor see him; then we are taken into his inner world. We follow Jeremy as he leaves his father, enters London's Bohemia, and finally finds a substitute father in Percy.

The novel opens with Jeremy playing piano in a London bar some years after World War II. A reporter from a London scandal sheet finds that he is the professor's son. From Eleanor's and Alfred's points of view, we learn that this incident is just one more example of the disgrace Jeremy's irresponsibility has brought upon them. Alfred is not quite sure how to respond. He knows that his father would have condemned Jeremy and preached hell-fire and damnation, but that will not work now. Eleanor, equally ineffective, tries to protect Alfred from shame.

Jeremy's story begins when he falls off his bicycle after trying to ride and study Greek at the same time. He ends up on the grass on his back, and the Greek grammar ends up in a fish pond. To Jeremy, the lost book represents a symbolic revolt against Alfred's philosophy. He vows to leave behind him Alfred's way of life and to engage life for himself. True to his vow, at the end of the school term Jeremy runs away. He spends some time on a farm, then goes to London, where he finds a job as a pianist in a saloon. During this period he meets Diana—a local prostitute—and Tim—a London draft-dodger. Diana exposes Jeremy to the seamy side of London life, and Tim provides Jeremy with false identity cards, enabling him to avoid the draft.

In contrast to Jeremy's story, Alfred tells of how he had

volunteered for the First World War, had been full of fear, but had persevered until wounded at Vimy Ridge. During this time Alfred found a foster father in Major Edwards, a man who is worshiped by all of the young officers in his outfit. We learn that Alfred had not gotten along well with his own father, a Victorian clergyman who campaigned against the ungodly and who called with religious fervor for more slaughter in the war against the Huns. After the war, Alfred adopts an atheism in which duty and service to others are the virtues, but in which Major Edwards is the Christ figure to whom he prays for intercession.

Although Alfred tries to instill this faith in his son, Jeremy revolts. To him, World War II is a tiresome inconvenience connected with blackouts and rationing. The only good part of the war is that it brings him into contact with American jazz musicians, among them Percy Brett — a black blues trombonist in the United States Air Force. In him Jeremy finds a gentler, more personal advisor than Alfred ever found in Major Edwards. It is in the different needs of the father and son, in the experiences of the two men, and in their attitudes toward war that Wain manages his implicit comparison of the two generations.

Ironically, the more Jeremy defines himself in opposition to his father, the more circumstances force him to perceive similarities. At the end of the novel, he understands that although he began playing jazz in the 1940s, the 1950s is the era of rock and roll. Jazz, to Jeremy's surprise, has become as esoteric a discipline as Greek. "I saw now," observes Jeremy in the final pages, "that my way was really the same as the old man's. You played music, as you studied the classics, because you had chosen it as your own particular skill, the contribution you were going to make, the thing you were good at."[4] After the war, both father and son come together in a kind of sympathetic understanding and mutual respect.

II *Critical Reception*

Critics received *Strike the Father Dead* with conflicting opinions. It was reviewed, on the one hand, as awkward, inept, tedious, and repetitious and, on the other hand, as powerful, poignant, serious, and mature. Such a variety of responses is perhaps not remarkable for a novel that departs from expectations and that attempts so much.

Some critics found the book to be a disappointment because the author departed from the familiar. They expected comedy and were unsure how to deal with a novel which presents a more complex view of human nature and a subtler main theme.[5] Few critics questioned Wain's serious intent. To Samuel Hynes, the book was "a serious, intelligent, conscientious piece of work."[6] Malcolm Bradbury found its most pleasing quality to be "a warm, documentary reality."[7] Several critics praised as superb its evocation of the general jazz-playing ethic, which Wain penetrates with precise, clear social detail. His descriptions of Paris, however, lack conviction.[8]

Other critics agreed that in this novel Wain's characters have become more active and, psychologically, more aware of themselves. Mellown felt that Wain "commands an almost flawless technique and can write in a truthful, accurate, and revealing way about human beings interacting on the personal level."[9] James Gindin found Jeremy to be typical of Wain's later characters, all of whom "are more complex, recognize the strains of different elements of humanity within themselves, understand darker sides of experience that are not presented melodramatically."[10]

If the deepening seriousness the novel recorded elicited dismay from some critics, few denied its power. The most incisive criticisms of the novel are in agreement that the book is clearly written, and they further agree in their judgment of the plotting of that book. This agreement, in itself, is some form of tribute to the clarity with which this novel is written. Called a turning point by many early reviewers, it has in the intervening years consistently held a central position in most discussions of Wain's fiction.

III   Characterization

Strike the Father Dead marks a considerable advance over *Hurry on Down* and *The Contenders* in the thorough rendering that makes each character—and particularly each scene—significant in a way that did not always happen in the earlier novels. In this book, Wain is working with a small set of characters, and he has abandoned—temporarily, at least—the earlier convention of third-person narration. By employing a first-person, subjective angle of narration, he focuses attention more evenly on each of the figures. Had Wain limited the narration to Jeremy's point of view, the characterization of the other figures would have suffered. However, because of the alternating first-person narration, Jeremy is not the only fully realized character in the novel. Alfred and Eleanor are fully developed, too. The result is that we come away knowing Jeremy even better, because what we learn about him comes not only from his narration, but from other sources as well. Inasmuch as there are three central characters, *Strike the Father Dead* represents a larger range for Wain. Each interior monologue is a revelation: the language is personal, distinctive, and descriptive of character.

Eleanor, for example, combines with her appearance a strict, prudish morality, a narrow vision of what constitutes proper behavior. Her morality is based on the Bible, the Ten Commandments, on unchanging moral laws. The inadequacy of these laws is clearly revealed in the early stages of the narrative when she tries to inculcate Jeremy with a "moral sense" like her own. As Jeremy's moral mother, Eleanor attempts to shield him from and prepare him for the world. We hear her sensitivity and emotionalism when she says:

I didn't really know what I was crying about, precisely. It was all a mixture of things. The shock it would be for Alfred. The shock it was for me. The difficulties it would bring on us, having a scandal of that kind round the name of Coleman, a name Alfred has always carried high, like a banner. But more than anything else I was crying for Jeremy. Because I remembered him as a little boy with wide eyes, and a tangle of hair, and a snub nose and tiny little hands and feet. And I cried and cried, sitting there in the kitchen armchair with my half-emptied cup of tea. (p. 20)

Eleanor is definitely a fixed character in the novel, but she is charmingly, comically fixed; even when we grow impatient with her, as in her obsessive search for Jeremy, we sympathize with her because she represents the values of safety and loyalty.

Although Jeremy's mother is warm-hearted, the father's personality dominates the family atmosphere. Thanks to this austere, loveless man, the Colemans are reserved and formal. Alfred is bound to the happiness that comes by "hard work, the sense of difficulties overcome and a duty done. Rectitude, self-denial, and a quiet conscience" (p. 7). In the world in which he grew up, "a man was expected to do his work, and to go on doing it no matter what private misfortunes and discouragements he had to suffer" (p. 8). We hear Alfred's pedantic, rigid voice when he says:

At a foundation like ours, established in the nineteenth century with the object of bringing the light, or some of it, to the inhabitants of an industrial city, we are bound to remember that our particular traditions are those of austerity, industry, and an honourable poverty. Our salaries, to put it bluntly, have never encouraged the laying down of vintage port, and our *mores* in general are scarcely framed to provide the atmosphere within which an occasional over-indulgence seems logical and to be pardoned. (p. 3)

Alfred derived this philosophy from his father, a preacher who died wishing his son would take over in the pulpit. By 1910, however, Alfred knew that God was no longer a prime issue, so he substituted the Gospel of John for the *Symposium* and the classics. To Alfred, the world is "an adversary to be watched and to be controlled by discipline" (p. 27), and he tries to impose this attitude on Jeremy. Alfred detests jazz—something like "a disreputable private act, something like masturbating" (p. 40). Although he believes he understands Jeremy, he is ironically blind to Jeremy's needs.

It would be wrong to see Alfred as wicked, for he does what he believes is right. He disciplines Jeremy—or tries to—in the only way he knows how, and he gives him what he thinks is excellent advice for getting along in the world. But he fails to appreciate the consequences of his actions, and he fails because of his inability to judge himself clearly. Inasmuch as he is severe on himself, he is unable to see how hard he is on others. He cannot judge beyond the needs of his own ego. Consequently, Alfred has little if any understanding of Jeremy, makes no allowance for individual behavior, and provides no room for Jeremy's individuality.

As we shall see in the following section, of the three figures, Jeremy's character is developed in the greatest depth. We will also see that as with Eleanor and Alfred, Jeremy's discriminations are an index of his intelligence and sophistication. His language, too, is a revelation of character. His slangy, ironic speech is both a reflection and a criticism of his education, his environment, and his times when he says:

Only one thing used to worry me about jazz: the old man couldn't stomach it. I think the real motive for his persistent refusal to buy me a gramophone was that he thought I'd spend my time listening to jazz. So I would have done, too. He put his foot down—said there was a musical society at school, and I could get all the music I wanted from that, in a proper supervised fashion that wasn't allowed to clash with my serious work. I toyed with the idea of saving up for a cheap one, but my pocket money was so paltry that I knew I'd never make it; besides, I'd have to start saving up for records as soon as I'd got the gramophone, and I just couldn't face a *lifetime* of saving up. (p. 39)

IV Bildungsroman

In the manner of a *bildungsroman, Strike the Father Dead* is a novel which recounts the youth and young manhood of a sensitive protagonist who is attempting to learn the nature of the world, discover its meaning and pattern, and acquire a philosophy of life. Henry Thoreau, himself a traveler of some note, said in *A Week on the Merrimack and Concord Rivers:* "The traveller must be born again on the road, and earn a passport from the elements, the principal powers that be for him." In Wain's novel, Jeremy is a traveler—in London and Paris, and also in the geography of his soul. He speaks in terms that lift his wanderings from the level of the merely picaresque to that of a sensitive and insightful commentary on twentieth-century life. We come to understand what motivates Jeremy to revolt against his father and to run off to London. We share his experience, his apprehension of life. And from this narration develop some of Wain's major themes, including a preference of country over city, a respect for the dignity of man, and an affirmation of life.

Setting plays a vital role in this odyssey. It creates the time and place and also develops and expresses the feelings of the characters. The provincial and London backgrounds and the accurate rendering of the language make the novel come alive: one of Wain's most praised skills is his ability to depict the everyday, realistic details of life and to give a convincing picture of country and city life. Wain creates the texture of university town life and life in London and Paris by exacting description. Like Dickens, he is interested in the bizarre surface of the contemporary world, but in Wain's novel, we move between two contemporary worlds—a world of rigidity and repression, represented by Alfred, and a world of creativity, international and free, represented by London and Paris. The first world oppresses Jeremy; the second attracts and draws him. He dreams about it and invents fictions about it. Central to this new world is Jeremy's love of jazz. For him, the experience of jazz means beauty, joy, life, growth, freedom, ecstasy—the very qualities he finds missing in the routine, disciplined life of Alfred.

Throughout much of the novel, Jeremy deliberately defines himself in opposition to his father. "I wanted, actually *needed*," says Jeremy, "to think of myself as a rebel, bravely acting out a pattern that was the reverse of what I had been taught, experimenting with an upside-down and inside-out system of values" (p. 265). Jeremy seeks to escape from "*that* house, where it was so dark and stuffy that you felt not only indoors but buried" (p. 33). He sees the "endless round of duties and responsibilities that had been palmed off on [him]" not as life, but as a fraud (p. 38). Jeremy tells us later, "All I could do was to get away from the things that had influenced me, as I had already got away from my father. It was all part of the search for an identity and a way of life" (p. 260). Therefore, the course of Jeremy's life is a central concern to us as we follow him through successive phases of growth.

The obverse of this repressive world is the dream of release and recognition, of power and glory. Hence, the theme of death and rebirth unfolds in a series of initiations. Jeremy is forever attempting to find a new life, a fresh start: through the course of his journey away from home he assumes a variety of roles. Eventually, under Percy's direction, Jeremy comes to use his hands, to love music even more deeply, and therefore to begin to realize his hidden identity. Percy's symbolic association with the father figure, the ideal, natural parent, is suggested throughout the story.

"The traveler must be born again," said Thoreau; and Jeremy's voyage is a series of rebirths in his search for identity. His first enlightening moment occurs just before he tears up his Greek grammar book—the book representative of the way of life into which Alfred had tried to lead him. At that moment, the spell of the countryside begins to work:

The grass was soft and full of life between my fingers. . . . A few insects zoomed about in the mid air. *Life!* I thought. I didn't think anything more coherent; nothing you could make into a connected sentence. It was just that one word, *life,* that started beating around in my head, my chest, my belly, and finally my arms and legs. (p. 36)

For the first time, Wain indulges in a technique which he will subsequently use more often: the development of a correspondence between nature and human event and attitude. Like Jeremy, the grass is "young and tender" and wanted "to be left alone to grow and enjoy life in its own fashion" (pp. 35, 36). In direct antithesis to the atmosphere of moral restriction which pervades the Coleman home, Jeremy finds the freedom which the outdoors provides. Inspired with a new appetite for living, Jeremy rushes home, plays the piano, and experiences "a blessed sense of release" (p. 38). The sound emanating from the piano is beautiful: "full of colour, life, depth. All the opposites of what [Alfred] was trying to push [him] into" (p. 41). Suddenly, Jeremy knows what he must do; he is hungry for reality.

Jeremy's next moment of illumination occurs when he meets a prostitute named Lucille. Jeremy had never before played piano in a public dance hall. He had never kissed a girl, drunk, or been in a fight. All of these experiences overwhelm him in one unforgettable evening. Naively, he sees all of this experience as an opportunity "to break out of the shell of a schoolboyishness and physical inexperience" (p. 64), but he ends up sick, beaten, and depressed. He has overestimated Lucille's glamour and has failed to realize that sordidness, violence, and primitive passion are realities as true as the beauty of music. The world, the wonderful world, to which Lucille introduces Jeremy is the world of saloons, with their drunkenness, roughness, cheapness, and squalor. The next day Jeremy is filled with self-disgust and self-condemnation, all of which leads to a time of temporary religiosity when he wants to torture himself back into purity. He says:

It was because I, with my youthful body, unlined face, clear eyes, had put myself voluntarily on the same level as raddled, ruined Lucille. I had felt lust for that disgusting body, and had given way to that lust. (p. 88)

For weeks he lives "in the world of prayer, self-discipline, and spiritual communion that the saints and mystics live in all the time" (p. 94). He experiences hell, but keeps struggling for the gift of life now, rather than the promise of a life hereafter. All along, Alfred and Eleanor ironically interpret his behavior as pure moral guilt, unaware that he is suffering from "physical and emotional shock" (p. 87).

This period of self-disgust is relieved when a sudden revelation brings him to a sense of reconciliation: a recognition of the value of living. Jeremy realizes that although he has behaved in a way he dislikes, loathing himself only leads to immobilization. He has imposed upon himself the very restrictions from which he had been fleeing. Thus, one day "this fervour of holiness, this mood of recoil from the physical world" (p. 97), falls away from him. This change occurs after an experience which extends his knowledge of life and develops within him more positive feelings about himself, his world, and his future.

One day during a cricket match he hears a dog's bark and sees a pretty girl. The sight of the young girl brings back to his mind physical, tangible beauty. He feels as if a girdle has fallen from him. "Lucille, the whole unutterably disgusting and frightening physical memory of Lucille, suddenly receded. That wasn't the reality of womanhood" (p. 99). It is the dog and the girl, in whom Life and Beauty as symbols are merged, that bring about the turning point in Jeremy's life, cause his realization and recognition of the missing element in his life, and lead to his enlightenment:

And because I loved them, I had to love myself. . . . The world was opening out before me, and it wasn't a world of punishment and penance, but of life. . . . I could find a place in my world for everything and everyone—yes, even for poor old Lucille. (pp. 100, 101)

From this experience, he realizes that London combines all facets of experience into a dynamic synthesis. He does not evade the violence, the evil, and the sinister; in confronting them honestly, he negates their influence in favor of the good, the beautiful, and the true.

A subsequently closer contact with jazz completes Jeremy's transformation. In London and Paris, Jeremy is educated to the complexities of life; no longer is he content with the simplifications of experience which satisfy Alfred and Eleanor. Meeting Percy Brett offers new dimensions to jazz he could never have guessed were possible. As he immerses himself into his career, he finds he has forgotten "home, family, the war, time, nature and death" (p. 133). His rebellion against Alfred has left him "with no roots, no history, no memory" (p. 203):

I felt I'd like to be Jeremy, but I didn't know who Jeremy was or how he would act. All I could do was to get away from the things that had influenced me, as I had already got away from my father. It was all part of the search for an identity and a way of life. (p. 260)

In *Strike the Father Dead,* the account of Jeremy's months away from home is by no means one of uncomplicated joy and happiness; as we have seen, Jeremy has his troubles, and sometimes his life is quite unpleasant. Yet the violence and fear, of which there is a considerable supply in the story, do not have the same kind of horror about them that we will find in the succeeding novels. The story is comforting because, for better or worse, Jeremy is growing up. He learns from his experience, and by the end of the novel he has an awareness of himself and his world. Jeremy's growth in perception gives Wain's story its lasting interest.

However, if *Strike the Father Dead* tells the story of a British young man who becomes successful, the success is to a certain extent bittersweet. For in his triumph over his home circumstances, Jeremy loses something as well. There are various names we can give to it: innocence; boyhood; nature; the secure, predictable life at home. The world beyond the academic life was waiting in the wings, and, all unknowingly, Jeremy was doing his best to bring it onstage. With it came a developing sense of injustice, deprivation, and suffering. These concerns will become focal points in Wain's subsequent novels, as he turns toward the impulse to define character and dilemma much more objectively and with greater moral responsibility.

V   *Conclusion*

Strike the Father Dead is central to the literary career of John Wain for several reasons. It demonstrates clearly the artist's ability to handle the expansive complexity of forms larger than the conventional picaresque tale. It exhibits the author's attempt to work more realistically with the materials than he had worked with before in grotesque and comic terms. It represents an increasingly pessimistic vision: the world of the novel is an opportunistic, career-minded world in which the hero must fend for himself. Finally, it reveals that Wain has improved his characterization, has sought to explain more serious themes, and has succeeded in the use of point of view and focus. It is clear that *Strike the Father Dead* is a transitional novel, one in which Wain tries—and succeeds—to integrate plot, theme, character, and setting. All of these techniques will be useful in his later novels.

Overriding these matters, however, we must consider the complexity of the characters. In Wain's earlier novels, the central characters were by and large passive, men who received awards because they accidentally or inexplicably did not attempt to bully or manipulate others.[11] But in *Strike the Father Dead* his hero is more assertive, and this assertiveness indicates a change in Wain's outlook on life. For one thing, life is more serious, more precarious, and less jovial in this work. The simple romantic fantasy solution at the end of *Hurry on Down* is no longer possible. Rather, in *Strike the Father Dead* Jeremy is surprised by the world opening up to reveal events unanticipated in his original vision. He finds that he must adjust to the society in which he has chosen to live. Most important, the novel does not end resolved: we feel that frustrations and challenges point ahead. In his next two novels, Wain moves on to broader visions of the individual struggling with the world.

CHAPTER 4

Human Alienation

WAIN'S next two novels disclose his readiness to set new and challenging problems for himself. *The Young Visitors* (1965) and *The Smaller Sky* (1967) are distinguished by a greater range of situations, by larger social and moral implications, and by a deeper pessimism. Although Wain continues to employ the form of the traditional novel—good and bad characters, straightforward plot, clarity, realism—the plot conflicts reflect Wain's more complex response to a more complex awareness. His world no longer allows carefree, predictable figures of fun to move about casually, relying on good luck and practical jokes to see them through their difficulties. Now, life can be sinister, savage, and pathetic as well as compassionate or comic. His characters are suffering, often lonely and tragic individuals, no longer masters of their environment. Each is in a hopeless situation with little chance for leading the good life, free of anxiety, guilt, and doubt.

I The Young Visitors

In 1960 Wain spent four weeks in the Soviet Union. That time, he confesses, became one of the formative periods of his life. His experience of getting to know, "by direct physical contact and absorption, what the day-to-day quality of life in the Soviet Union was like, quite simply altered [his] entire view of the world."[1] Up until then, he was very much unaware of politics. He went to the Soviet Union expecting to find something close to a liberal Western society. What he found shocked him and taught him to reevaluate all of his political experiences. He continues:

It taught me what totalitarianism even with its mild face, even with its mild expression, is like. . . . And I must say that it gave me a much more critical attitude to one generation that we have in the West, . . . who have been protected from totalitarianism so that they no longer know what it means.[2]

The Young Visitors was a direct outgrowth of that trip and is seen by critics as Wain's attempt to make something of the cold-war theme. Like *Strike the Father Dead*, it is written in personal monologue, this time from the alternating points of view of Elena (a contemporary Soviet youth) and Jack Spade (a professional literary Communist living in England). The novel is Wain's first imaginative work devoted to political affairs because his characters are in orientation different from his earlier figures. One reviewer commented: "His visitors are among the truest modern Russians seen by a novelist, and his best achievement is to make it exquisitely clear how their loss of faith in an oppressive system is not necessarily political triumph, but human tragedy."[3]

Wain himself has set out what he considers to be the dominant theme of his work: the book according to him attempts to deal with a Romeo and Juliet story of "two young people on either side of the ideological debate who fall in love and who are dragged apart because of their commitment, which is in fact a spurious commitment on either side."[4] Suggested here is a recurring theme in Wain's fiction: the innocent's initiation into awareness. The title is an obvious echo of *The Young Visiters* (*sic*), the 1890 novel by Daisy Ashford. One reviewer said:

It is the note of innocence and openness Wain wants to suggest, the innocence not of a child observing the cryptic events of the adult world, but that of a group of young people from the Soviet Union, observing for the first time the equally mysterious goings-on in Western society.[5]

The action of the novel is simple and straightforward; it covers fourteen days. Three young men and three young women, all Komsomol (Soviet Youth) members, arrive in London to study local government. Their announced purpose is to learn firsthand about the weaknesses and corruption of the Capitalist system. From Elena's point of view we take in what they see and experience.

Accompanying the youth on this educational journey is their superior, Comrade Olga Novikov. She is a well-seasoned Communist party member whose duty it is to shield the young visitors from the corrupting influences of Western customs. When Andrei proposes that they go to a movie to learn about Western attitudes, Olga responds: " 'To expose oneself to that corruption, indiscriminately, on the grounds that one is conducting an 'analysis' of Western customs. . . . The danger is obvious.' "[6] She suggests instead that they watch an interview program on television.

The star of the show is Jack Spade, a local who has developed a reputation as a professional public Communist. His defiance of capitalistic values impresses them. "Here, in this welter of falsity and decay, was a champion who defended the true values of life" (p. 27), says Elena. They are further charmed when Spade disclaims any personal possessions or comforts. Like the true Communist that he purports to be, his only satisfaction comes from knowing that he is helping to bring closer the day when the English people will be liberated and happy under Communism.

Spade's performance so entrances them that they decide to visit him at his headquarters—the Rebellion Cafe in Soho—where he presumably directs some theaterless actors called the Rebellion Theatre Group. In the meantime, we learn from Spade that he is not what he pretends to be. Rather, he is a cynical, opportunistic Communist who is in the "rebellion business" (p. 35) purely for money and comfort. Fast cars and fast women attract him. Currently he is living on the royalties of a terrible anticapitalist novel entitled *Leprosy,* which he wrote in ten days and had published in Moscow.

When the Soviet youth arrive at the café, Spade sees an opportunity for making a good impression on Olga. He hopes Olga will take a good report of him back to Moscow, which in turn will mean a healthy subsidy. Then he can drop his "mob and get some real actors, trained ones" (p. 45).

Olga's impressions are not uppermost on his mind, however, when he meets Elena, the sensitive, dark beauty, the most tender-hearted of the Russian group. All of his energies are directed at her. Elena is so impressed by him that she pays Spade a second visit later that night. Ironically, she has come to learn more about his movement, but he thinks she has returned for lovemaking. Much to her surprise, since she believes he has nowhere to sleep except on the benches of the café, he takes her to what seems to her a luxurious apartment. Eventually he succeeds in seducing her. Outraged and horrified by what she has done, she curses herself and admits her guilt before the comrades. Tipped off about Spade's real character by the local party secretary, Elena seeks revenge by pretending that she is going to defect to the West.

Because Spade is now in love with Elena, he is determined to persuade her to stay in England and marry him. But she, together with Olga and the other members of the group, confronts him and calls him a phony. Thus he has lost both Elena and any opportunity for a Moscow-paid career as an advertisement for Communist art. As a final irony, when they return to their hotel the youth find that Tastiana (the most dedicated of them all) has chosen political asylum in Britain. The students then fly back to Russia, knowing they will be met not by eager friends and families, but by the grim interrogators of the party.

As the plot suggests, *The Young Visitors* is a combination travelogue and innocent-abroad story, love-in-conflict-with-love theme, and satire on the innocent girl visiting the big city for the first time. Wain is a writer belonging to a popular tradition, and behind the characters in this, in fact, exceptional departure from his work there lies much literary stereotype which he had to penetrate and which, in a sense, we have to penetrate, too.

The first of these stereotypes is Elena. She is the conventional, innocent young woman who accepts the assumptions of her society without question. Like Charles Lumley, she finds herself in an uncustomary setting, confronting people who treat her as a stranger. Also like Lumley, she resolves not to be assimilated into her new surroundings. However, the reason for such a resolve, and its marked difference from Lumley's uncertainty, is that Elena is literally a foreigner in England and therefore subject to an isolation much more total than the class barriers disturbing Lumley. And, because of her simple-minded zeal for communism, she becomes also the victim of a plausible, nasty man. Our sympathies are with her.

Jack Spade (née Vernon Prout), who manages to seduce Elena and then fall in love with her, is a second stereotype. He is a wholly conscious hypocrite who exposes himself with every word he utters. As the unsympathetic hero, he seems to be a parody of John Braine's Joe Lampton: "the lower-middle-class male to whom nothing matters in his grab for money, position, and sex."[7]

Spade then finds Elena's antitype in Olga Novikov. She is a villainous lady with a poisonous heart, the voice of convention and formality under strict Communist principles. We see her as a "dry, hate-filled, shrivelled little soul inside a tense, hungry body" (p. 165), full of bile; she is, therefore, "ugly", whereas Elena is "beautiful."

All three of these characters clearly enough crack their respective molds. On the surface, Elena suggests the conventional idealized innocent who has not been touched by deep experience in worldly matters. From her point of view, her progress is toward disillusionment. More important, Elena carries out several artistic functions in the story. Over half of the narrative is told from her point of view, and it is as the perceptive observer of events close to her that she is chiefly prominent. She reminds us of Charles Lumley and Joe Shaw, both of whom were able to detect fraud from a considerable distance. Elena shares some of their talent as she becomes the shrewd innocent who notices incongruities. At Spade's apartment, the dim lighting and soft music offend her. It seemed wrong to her, not morally wrong, but "stylistically wrong, so to speak" (p. 92). She has strength and responds with deep conviction when she sees her ideals corrupted. She is understandably indignant when Spade tries to seduce her. Although not by nature á calculating and designing person, she successfully seeks revenge against Spade after learning he is a phony.

Elena responds not only spontaneously but analytically as well. Wain exploits the assumed naiveté of Elena. His chief device is that of naive comment, innocently uttered but tipped with truth. The device is an old but an appropriate one. Elena, a young girl living in a restrictive society and ostensibly deferential toward the attitudes and opinions of the system or adults who compose that system, yet also girded by her own instinctive reactions, might be expected to misinterpret a great deal of what she observes and feels. Thus Wain draws a considerable fund of humor from the device of naive comment. Through Elena's words, we follow her as she is excited, puzzled, and disturbed by the strange life of "corrupt" Westerners. To her, England is the "home of imperialism" (p. 6). She watches as French students neck shamelessly on the airport bus. She sees "double houses"

(p. 11)—houses split down the middle with a blank wall and no connecting doors—obviously inhabited by the "decayed country gentry" (p. 12). She is surprised by the amount of traffic, unlike the unfilled streets of Moscow. Huge advertisements parading cigarettes and drinks shock her. "Nothing met the eye except gross, vulgar materialism" (p. 15). In her youthfulness, innocence, and sincerity, however, Elena forms a much-needed foil to Spade, whose nature and fortunes are alike so dark that, if unrelieved, they would threaten to make the early portions of the book even gloomier than they are. In herself, and in her honest attitude to her convictions, Elena serves to underline the hypocrisy of so many of Spade's attitudes.

Jack Spade is the complete antithesis of the innocent, sincere, direct Elena. He is the slave of the passions of the moment, often as unthinking as a child or an animal. This predominance of the emotional in his makeup is responsible for his violent swings from love to hate. He "worships" Elena when he believes she is physically attracted to him, but subjects her to harsh usage when she rebuffs him. In the earlier novels we saw the villains— Blearney, Philipson-Smith—from a distance through the hero's eyes. In *The Young Visitors* we see more than a surface treatment of the villain. Wain brings him up close: a little less than half the novel is narrated from his point of view. As a wholly conscious hypocrite, Spade looks forward to Adrian Swarthmore in *The Smaller Sky*.

Spade's most unpleasant business is the systematic seduction of Elena, without considering her feelings or convictions. His cruelty, charm, and greed make him too egocentric to avoid hurting Elena the ingenue, but not sufficiently so to prevent himself from falling in love with her. Although Spade's character is consistent and believable, his transformation at the end is not. The author's failure to foreshadow Spade's conversion from a manipulator to an honorable gentleman, or even to account for it, renders the ending inconsistent.

In addition, because of Elena's decency and vulnerability, Spade's character is made to look all the more sinister and unforgivable. His hollow world of self-promotion forms an amusing as well as effective contrast with the sincerity of Elena. Irony, of course, is everywhere. The truth of Spade is a mockery of his public image as a Communist. The entire encounter with the Soviet youth is an ironical misrepresentation of the facts. Spade's real motive of avarice is known to the reader from early on; his public position is a travesty.

The character of Olga, although not as developed, is a study of a heartless woman who has given total allegiance to the party. She rules with a firm hand and carries with her "the spirit of authority itself" (p. 18). Wain concentrates on her voice and appearance to indicate an essential inhumanity of character and a pervading quality of exaggeration or grotesqueness which becomes both comic and horrifying. Her voice is full of recrimination when she lectures Elena on sleeping with Spade. Her tone reminds Elena of "the scraping of two steel plates" (p. 132); it has "a cold, steely hardness" (p. 165). At other times she speaks "icily" (p. 162) or with a "mannish woman's voice" (p. 42). And her appearance is consistent with her attitude. She looks with "scorn in her eyes and nostrils" (p. 133); her face is twisted with "contempt, disgust, hostility" (p. 164). At another time her eyes look with "murderous calm" (p. 166).

As vile, unfeeling, self-centered, and grotesque figures, both Jack Spade and Olga Novikov are in direct contrast to Elena, and thus they gain our notice in their relation to her. Spade is perfectly willing to sacrifice Elena to his pleasures. Olga is adamant about sacrificing Elena to the mandates of the Communist party. Both Spade and Olga represent their respective society at its worst. They are symbols of—in Spade's case—decadence and—in Olga's case—suppression.

A study of the central characters brings us to one of the most significant features of *The Young Visitors*—the static quality of the characters. None of them changes very much. Relationships between the characters change—Elena in particular thinks less of Spade at the end, and Spade says he is in love with Elena—but the characters themselves go on in the same way. This static quality is partly a result of the duration of the action: because the novel covers only fourteen days, there is not the long period for growth and change we observed in Jeremy Coleman. More important, this fixity of character is central to the meaning of the novel. The Russian youths do not change because they are limited by the society in which they exist, the customs of which dictate their actions—approving or denying, aiding or stultifying. *The Young Visitors* portrays visitors from a closed world; there is no way to change, no way out, even, except withdrawal, exile (as

indeed Tastiana turns to). One of Wain's major assertions in the
novel, and one of his strongest criticisms of the Russian society, is
that it is constrictive; customs change, in history, but human
beings cannot. This is precisely the tragic quality of the world
that Wain alludes to in *The Young Visitors.*

II   The Smaller Sky

The Smaller Sky is similar to the preceding novels in that it
continues the appraisal of the antihero personality as a victim of
the modern world. Although Wain has treated the problem of
the nonconformist before, this novel is profoundly more
pessimistic than either *Hurry on Down* or *Strike the Father Dead.*
In it, two aspects emerge for the first time which distinguish
Wain's later work: first, a preoccupation with fatality, and a view
of events in the universe as being determined by a chance that is
usually malevolent; second, a representation of society as
indifferent and impersonal, caring nothing for man's efforts to
secure happiness. Indeed, Wain himself described the work as "a
symbolic *nouvelle* about . . . self-destructive loneliness."[8]

Arthur Geary, a quiet, middle-aged scientist, husband, and
family man, has decided that his marriage is a failure and that his
work no longer interests him; so he leaves his wife and two
children and quits his job. He takes a room in a railway station
hotel and spends his days in the station itself. Here he can sit still
or stroll about unnoticed, as he seeks some simple release from
the pressures of life. In the course of the action, however, the
hero is persecuted by all the forces of contemporary society that
must isolate, reform, or capitalize on the deviant. What sustains
him, and what he tries to encourage his son to appreciate, is the
belief that there is happiness somewhere in the world: " 'Life
changes, you know. . . . Every few years it alters and gets quite
different. No unhappiness lasts for ever. So all you have to do is
go forward.' "[9]

For a time, Geary's philosophy seems to work. He is calm,
capable, affable, contented with the acquaintances he sees in the
station. He is affectionate toward his ten-year-old son, who pays
him a worried visit. He is diplomatic with the psychiatrist who is
sent to talk with him. However, neither life nor Paddington
Station is kind to him. Belligerent figures step out of the traveling
masses. Doing no harm to anyone, he is forced into involvement

with layabouts, British Rail officers, interfering friends, a zealous psychiatrist, and a malevolent television journalist. Inevitably, in trying to escape from the television cameras, he falls from the roof of the station and breaks his neck.

As the above plot summary indicates, Wain condenses the scenic method of his earlier novels and works for the most part in short, disparate, fragmented, and rapidly shifting scenes. To bring Geary's story to its tragic conclusion, Wain develops the action from seven points of view: Geary; his wife, Elizabeth; his son, David; Philip Johnson and his wife, Julian; the psychiatrist, Dr. Maurice Blakeney; and the television reporter, Adrian Swarthmore. Wain limits his omniscience to one principal figure in each scene. Several critics felt that these shifts in focus diffuse any possible intensity that the narrative might have achieved;[10] however, this judgment fails to take into account that each change in point of view counterpoints Geary's plight. The seventeen shifts in point of view, together with the rapid cutting from one scene to the next and the sparseness in details or explanations, allows us to piece together the story for ourselves. As a result, we have the illusion of seeing a great deal happen in a short space. This method is effective because it enables Wain to maintain our interest; characters, events, and settings intrigue us and, as Michael Ratcliffe commented, communicate "a deep sense of pain, tact, and immediacy."[11] Moreover, the shifting narrative effectively mirrors the lack of wholeness or completeness in the characters' lives.

Along with the suspenseful plot, what we find most rewarding in the novel is the psychological insight into Arthur Geary. Thoreau's remark that "the mass of men lead lives of quiet desperation" could hardly be better illustrated than it is by this portrait. As an account of an outsider, a lonely and alienated man, *The Smaller Sky* has an affinity with numerous contemporary works. Seeking anonymity and some simple release from himself and others, Wain's protagonist suffers from some of the same middle-class discontent found in Amis's *That Uncertain Feeling*. Like John Lewis, Wain's hero is a man baffled by and unable to explain the world surrounding him. William Trevor saw Geary as the "lone figure" recurring in contemporary novels who is "saddened and maddened by the creeping threats of our bleak age."[12]

As readers, we are able to observe the hero "like guilty but compassionate eavesdropper[s]."[13] We share his soreness after he is beaten up, we hear the pounding of his fantasy drums whenever the pressures mount, we fear as he fears, and we reject as he does, too. Noteworthy, also, is that Geary is more slowly and subtly revealed to us than were the earlier characters. Wain presents him in a variety of ways: by describing him directly, by allowing us inside his thoughts, by showing him through the eyes of other characters, and by having others discuss him. All of these devices give us a more complete view of him than was possible in the other novels—with the exception of *Strike the Father Dead*, in which the principal figure is seen primarily from within.

Adrian Swarthmore is the complete antithesis of the good, moral, somewhat passive Arthur Geary. Insolent, insensitive, greedy, his personality completely dominates the scenes in which he appears. David sums him up accurately as "smoothly domineering" (p. 92). He reminds us of the masterful, selfish Jack Spade in the way he rides over others' feelings. He, like Spade, is a womanizer and a conscious hypocrite who condemns himself every time he speaks or thinks.

Uppermost in Swarthmore's mind are self-promotion and power. He wants his own television show, and he will exploit Elizabeth's confusion and Geary's vulnerability to get it. His own words and thoughts give him away, and we see that he is malevolent both publicly and privately. His appearance, like his pretended humanity, is artificial. He uses faces to impress his sincerity like a rubber stamp: when he approaches his boss, Sir Ben Warble, he practices his "sudden, dazzling smile" (p. 43). He has mastered the art of interviewing to the point that whenever he talks with a person, he focuses his attention on him as if he is the only person in the world. He is, in effect, a confidence man who succeeds in maintaining his deceptive role. He deceives everybody except David and the reader.

Of special interest to us, also, is the relationship between Geary and his son, David. Up until now, most of Wain's attention has focused on the absurdities and complications of the adult world. In *The Smaller Sky*, Wain sets himself the added difficulty of working within the more limited consciousness of a small child; the problem is that David sees more than he understands of his experience. To contrast David's innocent world and the adult's world of deception and hostility, Wain intersperses

David's thoughts with the other narration. Like Elena, David is a shrewd observer. He notices when his mother is upset, he knows that his father is afraid, and he correctly senses that Swarthmore is attempting to take advantage of Geary's absence from home.

Wain portrays David with warmth and understanding and shows special concern for youth and its despairs. Unlike Swarthmore, David pursues his father both out of love and out of a wish to protect him from unforeseen accidents or potential enemies. The special quality of David's characterization depends upon the skill with which Wain manages to make the objective reality of the situation that confronts David—the characters of the father and mother and the relations between them—quite clear to us and at the same time does not violate the limits of the small boy's understanding. The primary interest of this subplot is in David's character, in the mixture of ignorance and insight, naiveté and cunning, egotism and need for affection that make it up.

Related to David's character is the significance of the ducks upon which he muses. The scene is important enough to justify quoting it in detail:

He often went to feed the ducks on the circular pond in the park. The pond was close to the river and sometimes the ducks went to swim in the river for a change, but they always came back to the pond. When he was very young, people had taken him to feed the ducks, but now he went by himself. He kept a bag in the kitchen and collected crusts and stray pieces of bread and cake; he was in command of the whole operation. . . .

Why was it so much fun to feed the ducks? They fought and dashed for the bread as he threw it to them. Sometimes he would decide that a certain one was not getting enough; the quicker or fiercer ducks were taking the bread from under its nose. Then he would begin to aim all his bread at that one bird. If it kept missing he would cunningly throw several pieces of bread to make it move in a direction of its own, away from the others where it would have more chance. By tossing bread to one side of the duck you could make it go to that side. It was like moving one piece on a chess-board. Or like God. God could take one person and move him this way with an illness or that way with a happiness. When you moved one duck from among the others you did it to be kind. But you could do it to be unkind if you liked. You could move one duck all over the pond and always throw the pieces of bread a little too far ahead so that it never got anything to eat, just kept on moving and moving. God could do that if he liked. But ducks didn't know how to pray. If they could pray what would they say?

He was like God but he would be kind. The ducks would get to know him and they would realize that when David threw them bread it was so that they should have it to eat, and not just to move them about. And so in one small spot of the universe, one round pond with stiff reeds, kindness and justice would rule. (p. 22)

On one level the pond and the ducks function as a contrast to the tension and anxiety David feels at this particular time in his life. David is a sensitive child, a deep thinker. Although he hates his life, he finds comfort in his father's assertion that life will not always be without kindness and justice. His feeding of the ducks is an attempt to experience a little of that kindness and justice. Symbolically, therefore, the ducks are central to the novel, for they ultimately treat a boy's attempts to come to terms with some of the mysteries of life. A central mystery about life is the reason for this unhappiness and injustice. Like the ducks, Geary is essentially a victim. Almost a story-within-a-story, David is initiated into the nature of evil, and he tries to find some way of coming to terms with his discovery.

Along with the suspenseful plot and intriguing characterization, the novel is readable because it is the working-out of Wain's concept of fatality that thwarts Geary's efforts to secure peace of mind and, ultimately, happiness. We see that the plot grows naturally out of the chief character's nature. Geary's desire for peace of mind, Robinson's concern for his welfare, Blakeney's professional curiosity about the man, David's love and concern, and Swarthmore's greedy motives provoke the twistings and turnings in Geary's life and therefore in the plot of the novel. These conflicting forces are clearly marked early in the story, and the reader is content to see them entangle and then unravel. Much of the action depends upon chance and coincidence, but as George Clive observed, the climax has "the right degree of inevitability."[14]

Setting is also essential to our understanding of the novel. The book is primarily a novel of environment, because the milieu in which Geary lives—stark, impersonal Paddington Station—conditions his immediate life more than any other factor. Much of the early part of the novel is given to description of the station, an indication of its importance to the story. The impression that emerges from this section is of a place of gloom and solitude; it is an Underworld which also is impersonal and unalterable, a limbo somewhere between home and country:

Hunched bodies, weary faces, everyone moving with the shuffling gait of one body among a thousand bodies, sealed in the loneliness of one head among a thousand heads. (p. 9)

Geary lives in this lonely world virtually isolated from any social pressures. Much of the significant action of the novel takes place there: the station is the scene of meetings, both planned and unplanned, and of many other incidents. At his discretion, Geary can sleep in the hotel, eat and drink in the various refreshment rooms, take a walk along the platforms, and select his reading materials from the bookstalls. What is more, Wain integrates the character of the station with the individual's state of mind. The grim, bare, coldly gray world of Paddington Station suggests the stark misery of Geary's emotional state. The rootless loneliness of the hero is conveyed by the manner in which he is depicted as tramping the station. Geary is like "a cork being carried by the tide" (p. 10). He feels "snug and safe among the crowds and the impersonality and the friendly, predictable movements of the human tide that swayed about the station" (p. 73). Elsewhere, we are told that the station "fit over his world like a protecting lid" (p. 141). The railway train symbolizes the restrictions of society from which Geary has fled (the trains are "huge, coffin-shaped" [p. 10]). Opposed to the restrictions of the station—and society—are the heights to which Geary climbs just before his tragic fall. The station is "neither a point of arrival nor departure," and that is the point.[15]

A discussion of plot, character, and setting brings us to the principal paradox in the story: that of the value of the human personality. In his sympathetic portrayal of Geary, the author defines the uniqueness of the individual; at the same time, he suggests that if we allow the individual his unique inheritance, he will fail as a member of society. There can be no conformity in uniqueness. Without conformity, society as we know it fails.

III   Conclusion

The Young Visitors and *The Smaller Sky* offer a bitter

commentary on the plight of man, for they expose the disappearance of a sense of justice from common life. What is more, in his examination of loneliness, Wain has given us no answers; the resolutions bring us to the verge of despair. From this sad outlook, however, he created two memorable novels which, pointing as they do to the universal prevalence of sadness and loneliness, indicate a truth which no improvement in material or social conditions can alter.

In both novels, Wain's fiction is about special social problems. He seems to be using the novel as a conscious means of expressing a dissatisfaction with social or moral conditions. He sees the novel as a means of making people aware of these problems and perhaps of changing them. Both novels depict characters caught in loneliness and despair, with no possibility of movement from bondage toward freedom, from isolation toward love.

Although bitterness is quite apparent in Wain's next two novels, it is tempered by the compassion and understanding which the author shows for the heroes. The tension is that of love versus loneliness, and it is love, or rather loving, that wins out in the end. In *The Young Visitors* and *The Smaller Sky* the desultory attempts of the characters to fill the void are ultimately futile, whereas in his next novel some of the characters manage to fill the void by loving.

CHAPTER 5

The Remoteness of Love

WAIN'S most recent novels—*A Winter in the Hills* (1970) and *The Pardoner's Tale* (1978)—continue and elaborate upon many of the central themes of his fiction, but they surpass the earlier fiction in richness and complexity. Both novels exhibit, far more than do his earlier writings, an interest in the tragic implications of romantic love; and the greater complexity in character development allows Wain to portray fully men whose loneliness borders on self-destruction. Each novel is not simply another story of isolation or spiritual desolation, although it is of course that. Clearly each hero is cast into a wasteland, and the novel in a sense is the story of his attempts to find the river of life again, or possibly for the first time. One of the themes that develops from this period in Wain's career is that personal relationships are the most important and yet most elusive forces in society.

I A Winter in the Hills

With its setting in Wales, *A Winter in the Hills* marks Wain's departure from his first seven novels, all of which are set in the English way of life. The story expresses, perhaps more comprehensively than any other, Wain's feelings for the provincial world, its cohesion and deep loyalties, and its resistance to innovation from outside. Furthermore, it is Wain's most ambitious presentation of the sadness of contemporary alienation.

The plot is characteristically straightforward. Roger Furnivall, a middle-aged philologist whose life until now has been rather aimless and pointless, takes a leave of absence from his university post for an extended visit to North Wales. There he seeks to learn enough of the language to qualify for a position in the

Celtic program at the University of Uppsala, Sweden. His motives are not purely academic, however. With its encouraging supply of tall blond girls, Sweden seems to offer the most likely source of broadening his sexual activities.

Shortly after he arrives at Caerfenai, Roger hijacks one of the local school buses. This leads to involvement in a conflict between Dic Sharp, who has forced most of the local bus drivers out of business, and Gareth Jones, a proud, independent, and taciturn hunchback who refuses to give way to threats or blandishments. With his sense of justice aroused, Roger goes to work for Gareth as an unpaid fare collector to lend whatever moral or physical support he can.

Once it is learned that Roger has sided with Gareth, Dic Sharp and his henchmen try to scare him off. A pot of red paint is thrown at his front door. A wheel on his rented car is loosened, causing him to have an accident for which he must pay a stiff bill. His window is smashed, and his frightened landlady throws him out. Despite these and other scare tactics, however, Roger remains firm in his support of Gareth. He knows that if Sharp is unable to attain Gareth's bus service, he will be forced out of business.

Largely through Roger's efforts and courage, Sharp gives up, the buses are auctioned off, and most of them are returned to their former owners. The experience has been an important one for Roger. He has found hidden strengths. Bolstered by the dignity, loyalty, and love shown by ordinary people, he has discovered his own will to live as well as his own social and human value.

Also important to the novel's plot is Roger's love life. When his pursuit of an American tourist fails, Roger turns to Rhiannon, a Welsh beauty who works as receptionist at the Palace Hotel. Although cold to his advances, she assists him in moving to an abandoned and remote chapel in the hills above Caerfenai. There Rhiannon almost gives in to Roger, but the mood is broken when one of her childhood sweethearts buzzes the chapel with his radio-controlled scale-model Piper Comanche.

Far more serious to Roger is his involvement with Jenny, wife of Gerald Twyford—an economist at the local university. Convinced that Gerald is treating Jenny as nothing more than property, he persuades her to leave her husband and live with him at the chapel. Madog, a local poet who has written an epic about the exploitation of ethnic groups, helps Jenny to get a job until Roger and she decide where they can live together with her two children. At the end of the novel, Roger closes the chapel and prepares to take Jenny and her children back to London with him.

As the above plot summary might indicate, in this novel Wain goes further than he has before in defining and developing his basic concerns as a writer. Here we find his sympathy for the underdog, his respect for decency and the dignity of man, his affirmation of life; here, too, we find expressed Wain's deep interest in the causes and effects of loneliness and alienation. The length to which Wain develops these concerns is mirrored in some of the critical reactions to the novel. Deborah Linderman, Eric Moon, and Rosalind Wade, among others, recognized the success and importance of the novel.[1] The reviewers for both *Choice* and the *Times Literary Supplement* considered Wain's deeper insights into individual behavior his most important achievement.[2] A far more significant review was written by Robert Nye:

What is especially enjoyable is the rough-edged tenderness and kindness of Mr. Wain's concern, and the way in which he puts all his own resourcefulness as a story-teller in the service of reaffirming a handful of values which do not draw attention to themselves. He was always less likely to take refuge in irony than most of the writers with whom it was his fortune to be bracketed. He can now be seen in this, probably his most substantial achievement to date, as a realist motivated by care about small people and the way they live, whose care dares to find direct and unfashionable expression.[3]

The virtue of these reviews is that they point out a number of characteristics which distinguish *A Winter in the Hills* as major: (1) the hero is not a mere stock type or half-developed sketch, but a full portrait of a complex individual whose strengths, weaknesses, and needs are understood and vividly depicted by their creator; (2) action arises convincingly from the characters' dispositions; (3) there is a new distinctive grasp of the relation of the character to the environment; (4) the themes with which it deals are serious and important ones of concern to the reader; and (5) for the first time, Wain succeeds in fusing understanding and technique: it comes near to the balance of a work of art.

Our first inclination is to approach *A Winter in the Hills* as primarily a novel of character, the major interest and emphasis of which is the constantly developing character of Roger himself. Using third-person narration for the sixth time, Wain keeps the focus steadily on his main character as he progresses straight through several months that constitute a time of crisis in Roger's life. The limited omniscience of the narration never wavers, and little is learned about others in the story that is not revealed by Roger or by dramatic revelation of the characters in scenes with him.

Wain has three main ends to serve with his central character. He must make us see Roger's ordinary, everyday self and his habits of life, so that we can properly interpret his reactions to special events of the novel and appreciate fully their effect on him. He must then show us clearly Roger's special reactions to this situation as a measure of the psychological cost of a social conflict of this kind. Finally, he must make clear to us the social situation to which Roger is reacting, the objective, external conditions that constitute the problem. All these things Wain does within the terms of Roger's consciousness, within its natural range of perception, within the limits of its accumulated experience.

What we make out first is that Roger is alienated, unhappy, and without purpose. We learn this through his thoughts. His alienation is caused, understandably enough, by pain and suffering. We are told that in 1944, at sixteen, he lay for nineteen hours under *"a few tons of beams and bricks and rubble"*[4] left by a German V-2 rocket. There he listened to his injured brother, Geoffrey, the only other surviving member of his family:

Sometimes he sobbed, sometimes he cried quietly, sometimes he made no sound at all, and then at other times he lifted his voice up and howled, yes, howled like a wolf. His mind was going, but before it went he said goodbye to life. (p. 228)

Roger carries the tragic weight of this event for the next twenty years. When his brother dies suddenly, Roger finds himself without a reason for living. It is not surprising, therefore, that at the start of the novel we are told his life has been a "dream-like state of unreality" (p. 9). He cries within himself: *"I can't go on like this! Make room for me somewhere, let me live!"*

(p. 22). Yet his dead brother's hold on him is tenacious and crippling. Roger is ghosted by him; and only later, when he meets Gareth and becomes involved with Jenny, does he exorcise the past sufficiently to become uncaught if not completely free. Wain's sympathy for Roger—as an alienated, lonely man—not only prompted the theme of *A Winter in the Hills,* but also led him to make its implications explicitly clear by the quotation from William Butler Yeats's "All Soul's Night" which appears as an epigraph to the novel:

> He had much industry at setting forth,
> Much boisterous courage, before loneliness
> Had driven him crazed.

Also disturbing to Roger are problems with his own sexuality. Forty and unmarried (Margot, his wife-to-be, left him when Roger refused to abandon caring for Geoffrey), Roger seeks casual but intense sexual encounters. He realistically sizes himself up when he thinks:

He was no longer young; he was not rich; he had never been more than ordinarily good-looking. Such successes as he enjoyed were won by persistence and by never missing a chance. (p. 13)

While early on his drive is purely physical, we soon realize that Roger's needs are more deep seated, and that his pursuit of women is linked closely to his loss of Geoffrey. The frustration he feels is expressed clearly in a dream he has one night. Margot and he have argued about Geoffrey; she insists that Roger leave him and let him die:

After that, the dream became wild. Lust gripped them, and they slavered and bit at each other. Margot panted, "Wait, let's get undressed," but while they were snatching off their clothes a wall of plate glass grew up between them, thick and cold. Naked, they rushed to it, pressing with all their might to try to get some feel of each other's bodies through its implacable surface, . . . but it was no good, the glass was there, and from somewhere behind him, Geoffrey was saying, "I'm dying, Roger. I'm dying." (p. 84)

Only after he joins a viable present with a future is Roger able to transcend the past. In Jenny, he sees gathered "the whole of life, love, experience, hope" (p. 117). Like Edgar Banks and Catherine in *Living in the Present,* the moment Roger and Jenny come together is one of great healing and union. In this instant the grief-stricken man is made whole, his dead heart reborn.

Thus, as we are slowly brought in this way to recognize the shaken state of Roger's mind, we begin to measure for ourselves the effect on him of what he observes when he arrives at Caerfenai. Through most of the novel, Roger struggles doggedly against a combination of adverse circumstances, always in search of a purpose. Outwardly he forces himself on Gareth as a way of improving his idiomatic Welsh. Inwardly he "needed involvement, needed a human reason for being in the district, not just poring over Welsh verbs and weaving fantasies about Uppsala" (p. 68). The guilt he carries because of his brother's suffering and death helps to propel him into a more active engagement with contemporary life. His conflict with Dic Sharp draws him out of his own private grief because he is helping not only Gareth, but an entire community of people:

If they really managed to hold out until Dic Sharp was forced to sell, a whole network of small businesses might go back to their original owners, and the tide of creeping anonymity would be held back, perhaps for years. He squared his shoulders. He had some value, after all, in the life of these people. (p. 214)

We learn about Roger's character in other ways, too. As we have come to expect from Wain's other work, the main devices of characterization in *A Winter in the Hills* are verisimilitude of dialogue, inner thoughts, an unerring sense of the appropriate in physical details, gesture, and bodily movements. There is a further fictional device, used occasionally in *Strike the Father Dead, The Smaller Sky,* and elsewhere, but of paramount importance in this novel in creating a hold on the reader: his use of setting to reveal and reflect the protagonist's emotions and mental states.

For example, Roger's walk in the rain down the country roads, as he attempts to resolve his bitterness and disappointment from Beverley's rejection of him, is vividly depicted. It carries conviction because Roger's anxiety has been built up gradually and artistically. The pastoral world is a perpetually shifting landscape, and Wain depicts its shifts and contrasts with an acute eye for telling detail. Especially striking are the sketches of evening coming on in the Welsh hills, with their rocks and timber and vast expanses of green. Such descriptions help to convey Roger's yearning for happiness in a world which seems bent on denying him any:

Now the grass was sombre, its green lowered almost to grey; it seemed to draw light into itself and hold it, draining from the sky what little colour still seeped round the raw edges of the clouds. At the far end of the valley, where the higher mountains began, the grey stone slopes and densely heaped screes were suddenly menacing. Below him, the river wound rapidly through the valley as if hurrying to merge itself in the sheltering sea, that sea which now, as he turned slowly in a circle, his eye searching for Beverley, he saw spread out before him on the western horizon like a sheet of lead. Everything was battening down, rejecting light and warmth. It was lonely, cold and anti-human, so high up. (p. 17)

Unhappily alone and pining for attention, Roger is indeed parallel to the Llancrwys setting. While such passages may arouse in the reader little hope for a happy outcome, the writer's artistic integrity constantly balances the recurring mood of despair with a more hopeful mood. For Wain's power of minute observation is equally evident in the promising aspects of life:

The sun broke free of the mountains and prodded a long finger of light down towards Roger. Everything was new-minted, gilded, ringed with an entirely beautiful fire. On the wicked, on the weak, on the sensual, on the broken and disappointed, on every man and woman and bird and animal the sun would shine, and the wind would breathe, that day. (p. 85)

Thus a considerable part of Wain's art is to link the appearance of the landscape to mental states. We are struck by the compatibility of setting and character not only in *A Winter in the Hills*, but also in William Wordsworth's *Prelude*, from which the second epigraph to the novel was taken: "The solid Mountains were as bright as clouds." The life Roger explores, despite its evil and treachery, is still daring and redemptive, not just sodden, mean, and self-destructive.

With Roger's everyday self established, with his reactions to the situation clarified, we can now turn our attention to the wider social implications to which Roger is reacting. One major theme of the book is the invasion of the peaceful, conservative world of Wales by outsiders who have no roots in the region, and therefore no real concern for its inhabitants. These invaders are characterized by a sophisticated corruption that contrasts sharply with the unspoiled simplicity and honesty of the best of the natives. A related theme is the decline of the town: its economic insecurity, its struggle to resist the progressive and materialistic " 'cruelty, greed, tyranny, the power of the rich to drive the poor to the wall' " (p. 191). Through Roger's point of view, Wain expresses his opposition to the pressures—economic, political, cultural—that seek to destroy the Welsh and by implication all minority enclaves.

No discussion of the themes of A Winter in the Hills can be complete without a glance at the characters surrounding the hero of the book. The cast is large; what is remarkable is that while Wain was creating his picture of Roger Furnivall and rendering alike his inner and outer character, he was also creating a whole series of smaller sketches and vignettes, each in its given frame and appropriate medium. Masterly indeed are the women—Mrs. Arkwright, the English lady engaged in a running battle with local authorities in an attempt to get her garbage collected at her door; Beverley Jones, the American tourist who disappoints Roger; Rhiannon, the Welsh beauty who works at Caerfenai's only hotel and helps Roger find a place to live; Mrs. Pylon-Jones, the suspicious, easily frightened landlady; and Mrs. Jones, Gareth's mother, the dedicated, stoical woman who, in spite of her blindness, never complains but rather speaks for the strenuous, hard-working, dedicated people of the land. Jenny Twyford is the other significant woman in Roger's life. Typically, she pays a visit to the husband that she deserted when her children ask for their father. She is a mixture of sympathy and straightforward honesty; a loyal, intelligent woman, without guile or selfishness, though with her fair share of feminine vanity.

Like the women, the men—Gareth Jones, Mario, Ivo and Gito, and Hywel Jones—are fully realized, too. Gareth, of course, is tough and tenacious; his torso is as "broad as a bull's" (p. 30) and his face, "even in relaxation, [looked] as if it had been blasted out of rock" (p. 30). The Italian Mario runs a pub in Caerfenai; he is more fiercely revolutionary, more determined on home rule, than most of the Welshmen. Brothers Ivo and Gito, friends of Gareth and onetime bus owners themselves, "looked strong, hard; inured to evil and fatigue, tanned and roughened by the weather" (p. 53). Hywel Jones, whose bardic name is Madog, is writing an epic poem in Welsh on the Cherokee Indians (whose plight he sees as analogous to that of the Welsh). From the descriptions of these and other village characters, it is obvious that Wain cares about the smaller people and the way they live.

The only truly hateful characters are Dic Sharp and Gerald Twyford, and by the end of the book Wain has set them down with such sharpness that we detest them thoroughly. Sharp's contempt for his fellow humans, his vanity, and his arrogance are revealed to us in stages. As an acquisitive and predatory individual, wholly self-absorbed and parasitical, he reminds us of Jack Spade in *The Young Visitors* and Adrian Swarthmore in *The Smaller Sky*. His evil nature contrasts sharply with the unspoiled simplicity and honesty of the best of Welshmen. Also detestable is Jenny's husband, Gerald, a well-to-do academic politician with social aspirations. He spends much of his time in London meeting the proper people and exhibits the kind of shallow academicism generally distrusted by Wain. As a husband, he is sexually cold and makes no effort to provide Jenny with warmth. As an elitist, the Welsh language suggests to him " 'everything that's restrictive and old-fashioned and a nuisance' " (p. 61). Like Sharp, this character lacks the maturity and the contact with the past that we admire in the Welshmen.

In many important matters, Roger, Gareth, and Ivo and Gito, among others, affirm a nostalgia for the primitive and a belief that the elemental life of the country is infinitely superior to that of the city. Characters established securely on the land are shown to be hard-working and good-hearted. From their mouths come pessimistic judgments damning the social forms that help make men less than fully human. Here are a few examples:

This was what nineteenth-century puritanism, the refusal to countenance anything more entertaining than a Chapel sermon, had led to. Not to piety, not to theological study, not even to poker-work and tatting, but to frozen dinners and commercial television. (p. 21)

Economic forces were like forces of nature: they worked impersonally, but they manifested themselves through individuals. Small businesses, local services controlled by local men, were doomed everywhere in the world. Gareth was doomed; all the Gareths of the world were hastening to extinction faster than the flightless rail or the white rhinoceros. (p. 52)

Where was that race of men who could build a masterpiece in rough-hewn stone? Dead, vanished, and their successors had the marrow sucked from their bones by the dishonest paltering world of modernity. Unreality, substitute, falsity, compromise everywhere. (p. 58)

The effect of Dic Sharp, and all the men of his generation who were similarly minded, would be first to make the world into a chromium-plated desert, and then hand over that desert to their unspeakable offspring. (p. 162)

In a world as it was becoming, violence of any kind was one of the commonplaces. Already, people in half of the cities of the world were afraid to go out at night. (p. 259)

Roger's critical responses cited above spring from a fund of assumed values, including sincerity, simple decency, tradition, and a respect for whatever survives of inherent dignity in human beings. During his wanderings around North Wales, he runs into walls that separate people—from each other and from them-selves—and shut out love. In his search, he seeks not only a reality uncontaminated by thoughts of Geoffrey and Margot, but also acceptance, stability, a life embosomed upon what is known and can be trusted.

Characterization, therefore, is important to our understanding of *A Winter in the Hills*, but Wain's novel is not merely about the growth of one human being from loneliness and alienation to mature and selfless love; it is also a powerful thematic novel about the quality of living, in which Wain juxtaposes man's individual existence against the encroachments of the century. These encroachments include bureaucracy, greed, and material-ism.

By the end of the story, kindness and love are, at last, real kindness and love, plainly given and plainly received. We have come finally upon a meeting free of the tension and combative-ness of what has preceded. The turn the narrative has taken is not dramatically momentous; nevertheless, it is a turn. We are left with these two—Roger and Jenny—in a relation of love and kindness: a hopeful, benignant ending after all.

II The Pardoner's Tale

The somewhat optimistic resolution to *A Winter in the Hills* stands in stark contrast to what we find in *The Pardoner's Tale*, Wain's most somber novel. In no other work by Wain are the characters so lonely, so frustrated, or so obsessed with thoughts of mutability, lost opportunities, and death. Depending on our reading of Wain, we might call this novel either his most cynical or his most steadfastly disillusioned.

The Pardoner's Tale is really two stories—(1) a first-person tale about Gus Howkins, an aging Londoner contemplating divorce, and (2) a third-person narration (the controlling narrative) about Giles Hermitage, an established bachelor English novelist living in an unnamed Cathedral town, who gets involved with the Chichester-Redferns, a woman and her daughter, while he is working out the story of Howkins. It is the interplay of these two stories which constitutes the plot of *The Pardoner's Tale*, and it is the effect of (2) on (1) which carries the theme, or unifying principle, of the novel.

The narrative begins with the character Hermitage creates, Gus Howkins, the owner of a British press-clippings agency, assembling his folding-canoe at an estuary on the coast of Wales. Howkins, in his forties, is four months' separated from his wife, whom he was pleased to catch in an extramarital affair. It provided the occasion for him to break up a boring marriage. "I knew, of course, that I was catching her out on a technicality,"[5] he says. So he is vacationing alone, satisfied rather to be "bored on [his] own than bored with her" (p. 36), and hoping for something better.

While canoeing, Howkins spots a lovely, but apparently dazed, young woman sitting behind the wheel of her car on a sandy spit slowly being enveloped by the tide. The car is lost to the sea, but not before Howkins rescues the woman and brings her back to his rented cottage, where in time they make love. But when Howkins awakes the next morning, he finds she has gone. He takes up the search, sensing that the woman would mean remission from boredom.

Meanwhile, Howkins's creator, Giles Hermitage, takes a break from his writing. He is a successful novelist in a small cathedral town, and on the day his story begins is agonizing over Harriet, his lover of seven years, who is at the moment somewhere in the air on the way to Australia with her new husband. Attempting to turn his mind away from Harriet, Hermitage decides to read three pieces of mail from his enormous pile of correspondence.

One letter is from Helen Chichester-Redfern, a woman who lives along the route of Hermitage's daily walks. She knows him from his walks and she has read his novels. She is also dying of cancer and wants to talk to Hermitage about his books, particularly the book he must be working on at the time. Through these talks, she hopes to use the writer's insights to make some sense of her unhappy life. Grasping at anything to interrupt his thoughts of Harriet, Hermitage telephones the house and agrees to visit.

It is there that he meets the daughter, Diana, a professional guitarist at twenty-eight. They strike up an affair. Meanwhile, with each successive visit, Diana's mother pushes Hermitage to discuss his feelings toward love and marriage and to explain why his books seem to show an antinuptial bias. Gradually, over a series of meetings, she reveals her own bitterness about her husband's long-ago desertion. In a deathbed request to which Hermitage reluctantly agrees, she asks him to get back at her husband by writing about a selfish person who comes to a mean end. Her wish is fulfilled in *The Pardoner's Tale*, although Hermitage did not originally plan it that way. Thus the rewriting of Howkins's fate.

Whether Howkins ends well or ill, especially with respect to his erotic involvements, depends on how well Hermitage makes out with Diana. The resolution of one plot determines the resolution of the other. As the tale develops, Howkins learns that the girl he had rescued is named Julia Delmer, a distressed actress who has fled her television-star husband after witnessing his gross sexual misconduct—involving two prostitutes and another man. Julia's unstable brother, Cliff, and soon the police, get involved when Cliff tries to swindle the husband with fraudulent ransom notes while his sister is away. Howkins falls in love with Julia and desires to take her away from Jake, her husband. This is not easy, however. She is a dependent woman, used to centering her life on the man she married; also, she has a sisterly, protective attitude toward her delinquent brother. Besides, Howkins has his own problems: an estranged wife who seeks reconciliation and a daughter in nursing training whose good opinion of him means a lot.

By the end, however, events turn sad. In Howkins's case, Julia returns to her husband. In Hermitage's life, Diana suddenly leaves him behind for an acquaintance he never met. Hermitage returns to his old girl friend—Harriet—and Howkins, brokenhearted, believes his life is over:

Now I knew there was nothing left but age, the slow dying-out of impulse, the cooling of the warm blood in my veins till it became thin, cold soup, pumping wearily round and round my body just because it had nowhere else to go, waiting for release and the end of pain. (p. 307)

What looks at first to be a rather disjointed story-within-a-story turns out to be, when studied more closely, almost a tissue of connectives. Nearly everything, we realize, is connected with nearly everything else in an attempt to explore the relationship between art and life. Each of the characters seeks through art some sense of order in a chaotic world: Hermitage (through his writing), Mrs. Chichester-Redfern (through her reading and her discussions with Hermitage), Diana (through her music and sexuality), Howkins (through Julia, the actress), Julia (through marriage to an actor).

Another unifying principle is that the book is directed *inward;* its essential setting is within the mind of Hermitage. The events that occur are seen principally through his eyes, and they have significance only as they relate to his inner nature. From the disarrayed writer perceiving the clouded sun through his open window, to the wasted figure in his little room hungering for the feelings, the momentary illusion, of personal well-being, Hermitage is apart and alone in many of the most memorable scenes.

Giles Hermitage is obviously the figure in *The Pardoner's Tale* with whom Wain is most intimately involved. He is a highly idiosyncratic figure with very recognizable weaknesses; he gets easily depressed (there is an early thought of suicide); and he resorts to excessive drinking. The root cause of his deathwish and drinking is loneliness. The early pages of the book, in which Hermitage meditates on his personal loss of Harriet, indicate this clearly enough. Like Edgar Banks, George Links, Arthur Geary, and Roger Furnivall, he is very much a modern man: vague in his religious and humanitarian aspirations; rootless and alienated from the social life of the community in which he lives; and initially weak and confused in his relationships with women.

Plagued by anxiety, depression, vague discontent, and a sense of inner emptiness, he seeks peace of mind under conditions that increasingly militate against it. Add to his problems the ever-growing urge toward self-destruction, and we begin to recognize in this novel a truly contemporary pulsebeat. Like the protagonist of Camus, Hermitage is a stranger in a world that does not make sense.

Unlike the earlier heroes, however, Hermitage tries to make sense of the world through the medium of his writing, by stepping back into what he calls "the protecting circle of art" (p. 228):

The only reason he had been able to contemplate the story of Gus Howkins was precisely because that story had been his companion through all the recent events in his life. It had gone along with him, step by step, providing an alternative existence that had strangely held to the same contours as his actual one. It had been a life-saving overspill; he had been able to write about the joy and sadness of Gus Howkins because they were closely linked to his own joy and sadness. (p. 311)

Hermitage's approach to writing is autobiographic, personal, subjective, even. The hero of his novel is a mask for himself. The author is creating a character who is his own predicament, and the agonies he endures provide a catalyst which enables him to express his deepest feelings about life. There are, indeed, several correspondences between Hermitage and the hero of his novel, Gus Howkins. Hermitage, like his fictional surrogate, suffers from meaninglessness and boredom with life. Both men are victims of the past. In each case, the afflicting circumstances involve a woman and unrequited love. Hermitage, like Howkins, finds some measure of comfort in a second woman, through whom, for a time, his sense of rejection and defeat is overcome. That Hermitage's own initials (G. H.) match those of his hero may indicate his sympathy with the sentiments expressed, too. In Hermitage, therefore, Wain presents a character who tries to create, as artists do, a new existence out of the chaos of his life.

Also of interest to us is Hermitage's life as a novelist. We see him as a detached observer of those around him (even his name suggests the life of a recluse). He is outwardly passive; we catch him at times overhearing conversations, lurking through his car window, watching people from a distance. Part of his separateness is his sensitivity, his unusual response to nuance and detail, to implication; he is almost hyperobservant. But he has also a great curiosity about other people, and he is an inveterate theorizer about their behavior. He has the notable gift for symbolic condensation through fragments of incident, bits and pieces of action, that seem to contain the meaning of a personality in a few words or gestures. We recall, for example, his thoughts immediately after meeting Dr. Bowen for the first time:

In the fifteen seconds it took him to get up the stairs, Giles considered the ginger-haired man. He was evidently in his thirties; well-conditioned; looked after his health, was pink and scrubbed; the slight overplus of flesh indicated only that if he had not taken such good care of himself, kept himself so trim and exercised, he would have been unhealthily fat. He exuded professional confidence. Ah! The doctor! Why was he still there at three-thirty? Answering the door downstairs? Acting like one of the family? (p. 74)

Then there is the period following Hermitage's introduction to Diana, when he thinks:

She was of medium height, slender in figure to the point of boyishness, wearing a plain dark-brown dress that would have been almost too severe but for a V-shape of bright checker pattern that started between her breasts and fanned out to the neckline. Shiny black shoes. Her way of dressing was obviously aimed at a neatness and restraint in deliberate contrast to the restless vitality that flowed through her limbs and issued in her quick, precise movements. Her legs, as slender as the rest of her, were unmistakably feminine in their elegance.

What else? Hair: brown, glossy as if with frequent washing and brushing, in a fringe coming down over her forehead, and framing her face: straight, with just the ends curling inwards.

Eyes: parsley-coloured; lively, enquiring, darting interested looks at the world.

Features: generally good; high forehead; mobile, sensitive lips; pale skin; the nose delicate and rather long, sweeping down her face and coming out into a pert, inquisitive curve at the tip. (p. 77)

By the time we have finished the novel, we know how a novelist thinks and feels, and we experience not only the writing but also its moments of inspiration, of perfected expression.

In addition to his habits of observation, another characteristic of the man is the remarkable abundance of literary allusions and quotations which filter through his mind. To begin with, we find implicit in the novel allusions to William Wordsworth's sonnet "Mutability" (apparent in Hermitage's reveries on the impermanence of all things) and to T. S. Eliot's poem *The Waste Land* (indicated by the time of the novel—April—and by Hermitage's "death-in-life" existence). Later, the narrator alludes to *The Myth of Sisyphus* (p. 73), to John Milton's *Paradise Lost* (p. 219) and "Lycidas" (p. 220), to Shakespeare's *The Tragedy of Antony and Cleopatra* (p. 264), to Bacchus (p. 232), and to Alexander Pope's "An Essay on Man: Epistle I" (p. 294), to name just a few. Wain uses these allusions not only to tell us something about Hermitage's interior world, but also to reinforce the themes of the novel. The reference to Cleopatra clearly defines the extraordinary sensuality and variety the hero sees in Diana's personality. The Bacchus allusion is merely playful, but the allusions to Milton, Pope, and Camus reinforce the theme of the novel: the vulnerability of human life, the inexorability of time, and the efforts of man through art, love, and fame to escape the destructive wheels of time.

The remaining major characters in *The Pardoner's Tale* bear family resemblances to those in other of Wain's novels. If the part of the lonely, alienated hero so effectively carried in *The Smaller Sky* by Arthur Geary and in *A Winter in the Hills* by Roger Furnivall is here assigned to Giles Hermitage, the role of the manipulator is assigned in this novel to Mrs. Chichester-Redfern. Granted that she is a good deal less ruthless than either Adrian Swarthmore in *The Smaller Sky* or Dic Sharp in *A Winter in the Hills;* nevertheless, she is a manipulator just the same, seeking to exploit the hero.

The process by which Mrs. Chichester-Redfern is gradually revealed to us through the eyes of Hermitage is subtle and delicate. At first merely a stranger, she comes to seem in time a calculating and educated woman, the innocent victim of a man who deserted her, a seventy-year-old woman grasping for answers to some vital questions about her own life. In a way that is unusual for him, Wain introduces his initial description of the woman in a letter addressed to Hermitage. Through the hero's scrutinizing eyes, we learn that she is respectable (the quality of stationery and handwriting connotes that), conservative and affluent (the address on the envelope indicates that), and well read ("She constructed her sentences like a person who has read Henry James" [p. 69]). These early hints about her character, however, hardly prepare us, or the hero, for what is to come.

In her ruin, Mrs. Chichester-Redfern is a saddening picture: depressed, helpless, terminal. Wain heaps images of deadness one after another to convey the total barrenness of her existence. The dying woman's face resembles "candle–wax" (p. 84); the skin is "tight over her cheekbones" (p. 75); her head is "fleshless" (p. 86); her body seems "as weightless as that of a dead heron" (p. 125); and her hand is like "the claw of a bird that had died of cold" (p. 180). Additionally, the repeated references to Mrs. Chichester-Redfern's eyeglasses as "hollow" or "dead discs" call to mind the eyes of T. J. Eckleberg in F. Scott Fitzgerald's *The Great Gatsby*. Like Eckleberg's eyes, Mrs. Chichester-Redfern's see in life only a wasteland, absent of love, faith, and the capacity for regeneration. She, like the doctor's picture in Fitzgerald's novel, looks out from the ashes of her past and onto the hopelessness of her future. Clearly this image further defines her situation.

Mrs. Chichester-Redfern has summoned Hermitage under the pretense of wanting to gain insight into the course her life has taken. From these conversations we learn that she, like Hermitage, is confronted and dislocated by external reality in the form of a personal loss. Also like the hero, she desires to come to some understanding of her unhappy life through the medium of art. Human loneliness is one of the main themes of the novel, and Mrs. Chichester-Redfern is the very embodiment of loneliness. She explains the source of her misery when she says:

"My life is over. Only my death is to come. And when I look back over it, what I see most is this great black shadow in the middle. The sun going behind thick clouds. Then emerging into only a smoky light. I have never been happy since my husband took his love away. And gave it to another woman. Diana has no love for me. When I conceived her. It was the effort of my whole body and soul. To keep him near me. I failed. She was born into a life from which love. Had been stolen. There was nothing. She has. Nothing." (p. 125)

With these thoughts in mind, Mrs. Chichester-Redfern says that she has summoned Hermitage to take advantage of his " 'wisdom and imagination, about human beings and the nature of their dealings with each other' " (p. 80). She wants to learn " 'why failure of love, separation, divorce, are such matters of concern to [him]' " (p. 80); ultimately, she hopes to know " 'what makes relationships succeed or fail, what brings happiness' " (p. 119).

While these early discussions are enlightening to us—they serve as the vehicle through which we learn the workings of Hermitage's mind in imagining his characters—they are not the real reason she has asked him to visit. Later she admits:

"I said that before I died I needed to make sense of life. To understand the things that had happened to me. That was all lies. I understood, all right. There's no mystery. Richard spoilt my life. I was a young untried girl. No experience of life, no wisdom, no skills, no profession, no property. All I had to give was my love and I gave him that. He took it casually. Laid it aside and forgot where he had put it." (p. 182)

Mrs. Chichester-Redfern's motive behind her summons is revenge, and she wants Hermitage to write a novel with Richard in it as a character:

"Let him suffer, let him know pain and then there will be that much justice done in the world. One tiny piece of justice against all the wrong and unfairness." (p. 183)

Searching the images of her past to see what significance links them, and intensely conscious of what she has made of her life, Mrs. Chichester-Redfern strives but fails to wrench some coherent meaning out of the flux around her.

There is a profound pessimism near the ending of the novel in which Mrs. Chichester-Redfern dies, alone but for Diana—who does not love her—and Hermitage—who pities her. The point of her story is that it is pointless; her death is as meaningless as her life:

The woman on the bed had struggled seventy years for happiness and fulfilment, and lost; and now it was all history, trivial anonymous history, the history of nine-tenths of humanity. (p. 234)

It is a tribute to Wain's skill that Mrs. Chichester-Redfern does haunt the memory once this book has been read. Although her life story is not particularly complicated, and although she has none of the conventional attributes of heroism, we feel her death as a moving personal loss. Indeed, Wain's evocation of the futility of her suffering is oppressively convincing.

In addition to the alienated, lonely hero and the manipulator, most of Wain's fiction has in it a comforter: Catharine in *Living in the Present;* David in *The Smaller Sky;* Jenny Twyford in *A Winter in the Hills.* In his latest novel, the comforter is embodied in Diana Chichester-Redfern. Unlike the earlier characters, the happiness Diana offers is only temporary. In this novel, love is reduced to a meaningless mechanical act: Diana, also, is living in a wasteland.

The basic tension of this novel is a simple and classic one—the life-force confronting the death-force. And as surely as Mrs. Chichester-Redfern is the death-force in the novel, Diana is the active and life-giving presence. She is depicted as an abrasive, liberated, sensual, innately selfish girl of today who stands in positive contrast to the deathlike grayness of her mother. Diana's physical description emphasizes her "restless vitality" (p. 77), her "preference . . . for the sunshine of life" (p. 114). In her company, Hermitage finds himself moving away from "the devouring presence-in-absence of Harriet," away from death to "sparkling life" (p. 115). She is earthy and fulfilled, accepting and contented with her music, her faith, and her sexuality.

Diana's music—she is a classical guitarist—satisfies her need for proficiency. She says, " 'I knew I could become an instrumentalist if I worked hard' " (p. 174). Her church, on the other hand, gives the girl her " 'bearing and takes care of all the serious side of life, all the moral issues' " (p. 174). What is more, she enjoys physical pleasure because she has no choice: " 'We're all helpless in the grip of sex' " (p. 135). Indeed, Diana goes from one affair to another, not in search of love (she claims she " 'can't love anybody' " [p. 239]) but out of a need for repetition. Diana defines love and meaning as the fulfillment of the man or woman's emotional requirements. To her, "love" does not mean self-sacrifice; rather, "love" is synonymous with "need."

Yet Diana is not melancholy; she knows her condition of life and does not hope to have life other than it is. Because she can live in neither the past nor the future, she lives entirely in the *now.* Her chief defect is that she is shallow. She lacks the imagination and compassion either to understand Hermitage's need for her or to comprehend the older man's misery. Her own emotions are always well under control; her affection swings

easily from Dr. Bowen (who is caring for her mother) to
Hermitage, then later to an anonymous man for whom she
deserts both men. In many ways Diana is like a scientist. All her
adult life she has been a collector of men. She looks at them,
handles them, acquires them, but she never establishes a human
relationship with any of them. Nor does she establish a human
relationship with her mother. Diana is too busy to dwell for long
on her death. It is simply one of many things she must deal with
as she forges ahead. "Hers was not one of those natures to which
compassion comes naturally" (p. 114).

Thus the world Wain's characters move through is, as I have
suggested, the archetypal world of all of Wain's fiction: random,
fragmented, lonely, contradictory. The Hermitage-Diana-Mrs.
Chichester-Redfern relationships, along with the subsidiary
involvement of these three with other minor characters,
intersect continually with Gus Howkins's story, each enriching
the other in complex and various ways. Structuring a fiction
(Hermitage's story) around a fiction (Howkins's story) provides
Wain with a suggestive form of enormous resonance and
flexibility.

The title itself plays on some of the ironic possibilities Wain
establishes in the interplay between art and life. It is a title
which obviously has numerous implications, none of which
necessarily rules out any other. For instance, every novelist in his
way is a pardoner, dispensing or denying hope to his characters
as the Pardoner in Chaucer's *Canterbury Tales* peddled
indulgences for the Pope. Wain no doubt had this in mind in
naming his novel-within-a-novel.[6] But he may have had more in
mind as well.

Perhaps Giles Hermitage is a pardoner: certainly, he brings
about the resolutions of Howkins's story in a spirit of forgiveness.
In light of Hermitage's search for death, we remember that
Chaucer's tale was also about a search for death. But we also
remember that Chaucer's Pardoner was a "full vicious man" who
could tell "a moral tale" and accused others of sin so that they
would guiltily buy his pardons. Therefore, might not Mrs.
Chichester-Redfern be the pardoner of the title? Perhaps she is
as vicious as Chaucer's Pardoner when she tells the story of her
life: certainly, she has no concept of forgiveness.

We should consider, for example, that Mrs. Chichester-
Redfern is a victim of despair, hopelessness, the occasion for

which is ultimately her affliction, setting her apart from the rest of humanity. Afflictions borne in patience lead to acceptance and to the love of God and neighbor; afflictions impatiently borne lead to resentment and to the hatred of God and neighbor. Mrs. Chichester-Redfern is, indeed, full of hate, both for the God who afflicted her and for mankind from whom she is separated by her difference. Thus she turns her gift of great intelligence into a weapon with which to attack the man whom she hates and despises. Hermitage is aware of her viciousness, her hatred; he realizes that she is a positively destructive force, far beyond his own anger and despair in its potential for wickedness. However we choose to interpret the title, the centrality of despair and the ways Wain develops it remain a basic part of the book's power and richness.

The Pardoner's Tale concludes, therefore, on a note of loss. In this respect it serves, as some critics have noted, as a contrast to the more affirmative conclusion to *A Winter in the Hills.* Through Giles Hermitage, Mrs. Chichester-Redfern, and Diana, we gain a sense of contemporary England as a wasteland. It is a world in which the action of the novel—wasted lives, debased sexual encounters, and destroyed moral selves—reflects a tragic vision of futility and sterility. Such traditional certainties as love, faith, and the capacity for regeneration have become remote and inaccessible. And alienation is the result. It is alienation in many forms: isolation from the community, estrangement from those who used to be closest to one, and loneliness in the midst of the universe itself.

One last point: the somber hues of Wain's latest work and his seriousness of purpose account for the small space he has allotted to humor—one quality with which previous works of his are especially rich. The farce of *Hurry on Down,* the amusing satire of *The Contenders,* the delightful rustics of *A Winter in the Hills,* have few parallels in *The Pardoner's Tale.* Wain was here too much occupied with his presentation of tragedy to be able to do much laughing. At times, however, he found it possible to slip back into earlier and more genial habits; and Chapter 10 serves, with its entertaining account of Diana's encounter with two clergymen, to show Wain's humor:

[Hermitage] looked covertly at Diana. She was at her most demure, eyes downcast and hands in her lap, but that tiny smile played about the corners of her mouth and he saw a glitter in her eyes that he had come to recognise as the sign that she scented a sexual challenge. The two clerics were holy men, but men all the same. . . . Diana reined in her sexual magnetism until they had finished the business of lowering her mother into the earth and were coming away from the graveyard; then she unleashed it on the guileless youth until Giles could have sworn he heard the blood boiling over in the victim's veins. (p. 255)

III   Conclusion

Since their publication, both A Winter in the Hills and The Pardoner's Tale have evoked a variety of commentary, respecting their themes, characters, and narrative framework. Most of the criticism on A Winter in the Hills centered on two strengths: (1) that Wain really knows the segment of Welsh life he portrays; and (2) that because he succeeds in fusing understanding and technique, the novel approaches the balance of a work of art. Likewise, reviewers noticed that while The Pardoner's Tale clearly belongs to the main tradition of Wain's fiction, and has a value apart from its subject and technique, in helping us to define that tradition, certainly its dark agonies make it his best and most serious achievement. And although several reviewers had reservations about its tedious, somewhat forced combination of two narratives, they all recognized its genuine power.

To Edward Butscher, for example, its power lay in Giles's tale "as he tries to deal with advancing age, the loss of his beloved to another man, the death of a woman who needs his complicity to die, and an abruptly terminated affair with the woman's sexy but unfeeling daughter."[7] Ian Stewart echoed this judgment when he wrote that Wain "has accurately and movingly analysed the sad plight of middle-aged men who fall in love with younger women."[8] Writing in the New York Times Book Review, Julian Moynahan said of the novel: "In his sober, serious way Mr. Wain teaches us to think more clearly about books, their makers and the fascinating people who read them."[9]

In comparing A Winter in the Hills to The Pardoner's Tale, we must conclude that the latter offers a deeper tragic vision of reality. What we are confronted with is a complex, finely constructed novel in which the main sensations are of failure: the failure of communication, of perception, of love. What remain most strongly with us are alienation, the inability to feel, and the loneliness of freedom, all of which are central themes in Wain's fiction.

At the same time, Wain is also close to offering one of the major twentieth-century solutions to the chaos of life—salvation through art. Proust, Joyce, and Woolf all offered this as an answer to the conditions Wain presents in *The Pardoner's Tale*. Hermitage's theory is an artistic vision for ordering experience similar in nature to Proust's vision in the last volume of *À la recherche du temps perdu*, when the narrator of that novel decides that only by recreating his experience in a work of art can he make it meaningful. It is tragic that Wain's narrator has not had and never will have this final vision.

CHAPTER 6

Other Fiction, Other Prose

IN addition to his novels, Wain has produced three collections of short stories and seven volumes of poetry, many scholarly essays, and a highly respected biography. Quite often these writings have been the principal source of his income and the support of his other creative work. About his literary output Elgin W. Mellown offered the following comment: "[Wain's] output (in both quantity and versatility) and its quality cause him to be reckoned an outstanding figure of his generation."[1] He has become, as Richard Hoggart predicted, a modern man of letters.[2] The term would seem to be appropriate to Wain partly because of his lifelong devotion to literature, a devotion which is simultaneously generous and discriminating, and partly because of his own formidable achievements in an exceptionally wide range of genres. There can be no question about Wain's erudition and virtuosity in describing him as an all-around man of letters. Not only has he written fiction and poetry which deserve a place of reckoning among his contemporaries, but he has published criticism which communicates a sensitive and scholarly appreciation of good books.

I The Short Stories

Consideration of John Wain's short stories is placed near the end of this study not because of chronological sequence (publication dates of the collections range from 1961 to 1972) but because we can appreciate them more fully in light of what we know of his novels. Not only do the shorter pieces recapitulate the central themes of the novels, but they reflect in their variety and in their unequal value all the pressures that went into the creation of the longer works. Critics have rated them high: they recognize that with Wain, the writing of the tale

108

is not just an intermittent refuge from the more exacting labor of novel-writing. Wain's creative energies and formal concerns are devoted in almost equal measure to his novels and his stories. Anthony Burgess, for example, remarked that whereas the novel form frequently hides Wain's fine taste and clarity of thought, "one can find few faults with his short stories."[3] Mellown, in his review of *Death of the Hind Legs and Other Stories,* found that "their content and form, skill and attitude [are] so perfectly balanced that they reach an artistic level [which] Wain just misses in his novels."[4]

Many of the stories were previously published in various periodicals such as *Argosy, Harper's Bazaar, Ladies' Home Journal, Reporter, Saturday Evening Post, London Magazine, Suspense,* and *Woman's Mirror.* They were subsequently collected, added to others, and published as three volumes: *Nuncle and Other Stories* (1960), *Death of the Hind Legs and Other Stories* (1966), and *The Life Guard and Other Stories* (1972). His short fiction covers the psychological thriller, the novelette, the extended joke, the psychological analysis, the simple character study, and the fantasy tale.

With few exceptions, these tales are told in a straightforward and uncomplicated manner, following the accepted convention of the dramatic presentation with a reasonable unity of time and place. Using either third-person or first-person narration, the prose is simple and colloquial. Usually the narrator is in a small line of business, rarely a factory worker or scholar, and sometimes a female. As a result of the events which occur, there is likely to be some rearrangement of the structure of his sensibility. Also, the stories are fixed in time by the convention of reference to things—the books, fads and fashions, brand names, and popular songs of a particular moment in time. The wit and humor we have come to expect of Wain in his early novels are present in many of the short stories as well.

Although somewhat restricted in setting, his short stories demonstrate a wide variety in subject matter, ranging from the treatment of a professional wrestler in "King Caliban" to that of the mature five-year-old child in "Master Richard," from the problems of a forty-year-old bank teller in "The Quickest Way Out of Manchester" to the interior world of a political refugee in "A Stranger at the Party." There is also a wide variety of moods, from the panic of "Darkness" and "The Life Guard" to the grim horror of "The Innocent," from the self-righteous respectability of "Down Our Way" to the nostalgia of "A Visit at Tea-Time." There is also a wide variety in time, for although most of the stories are set in the discontented present, some such as "Goodnight, Old Daisy," "Further Education," and "The Valentine Generation" look back to happier times.

Moving inside this frame of artistic control over subject, mood, and time, his short fiction reveals views and themes that are characteristic of his novels. Throughout the stories he is primarily concerned with the problem of defining the moral worth of the individual. As in his novels, we find here a constant assertion of the dignity of the human being. Moreover, his stories are often an exploration of what it means to be isolated and set apart. In story after story the leading character seems to be cut off from his world. His short fiction is thus peopled with aged Mr. Williams in "A Visit at Tea-Time" and Mr. Greeley in "Goodnight, Old Daisy"; by the drunken, once-famous novelist in "Nuncle"; by the dim-witted wrestler in "King Caliban"; by the very old and the very young in "The Valentine Generation"; by the frightened in "Darkness" and "The Life Guard"; by the suspicious in "Come In, Captain Grindle."

Yet those who are isolated are most often people who seem more valuable than the world that isolates them. The reason is that Wain treats their separateness with sympathy and even with love. In most of his stories, sympathy, gentle humor, and understanding mark the Wain treatment of many types of people. The isolation is what allows him to get inside his characters. Some are tragically treated, others comically.

If we begin with the first volume of stories, *Nuncle and Other Stories*, we find that the opening piece, "Master Richard," is narrated by a child of five who conceals his actual maturity of thirty-five years not only from his parents but from a world he has judged to be stupid and unworthy of honest emotion or thought. When his mother gives birth to his brother, Richard's ironic tone turns bitter: "I lie here twisting like a trapped snake. . . . This is the birth that should have been me."[5] Unable to destroy his baby brother, the young monster must take his own life because "nobody can fight against love" (p. 36). "Master Richard" is a dramatic tale and, although comic at the start, it ends deftly enough on a bleak note of tragedy. Like many of the protagonists in the novels, Richard faces a conflict between the real world and his deeper need for escape to another world altogether. In its fusion of poetry and outright horror, as well as the reiterated images of alienation and psychic crippling, "Master Richard" sounds curiously like Sherwood Anderson's tales of the grotesques. Moreover, Richard's need for revenge to even the score with a painfully unjust world reminds us of the short stories by Saki.

Less chilling but certainly no less memorable is Wain's second tale, "A Few Drinks with Alcock and Brown." Its examination of loneliness and alienation reminds us of *The Smaller Sky*. A young man, who "ought to have learnt how to run his life" (p. 38), tries to ignore a letter in his pocket from an ex-fiancée. Masterfully understated, tension grows through the young man's drinking at a bar, the senseless threat of a fight with a stranger, and ends with his obeying a "public duty" to inform the police. Thus, the letter is ignored for a while longer. Yet, "as he stood, glass in hand, . . . he thought of the first time he had kissed Ellen, . . . the only real thing in his life" (pp. 51, 52), and the portrait of a lonely young man is complete.

"The Two Worlds of Ernst," the third of the stories, is both a character sketch set in the Swiss Alps and an illustration of Wain's sympathy for the common man. The narrator relates the story of his friendship with Ernst, a man living apart from other humans but in tune with the natural world. He says:

His primitiveness and gentleness made a combination I had never met before in a European; and his rejection of artificial aids to living was so wonderfully thorough-going, an example of what *could* be done if you had a mind to it. (p. 56)

Two years later, however, Ernst has changed. He is working on a railway now and is about to get married. These changes have produced surprising results. "He had given up his own life, and walked into theirs as a stranger, or a just-tolerated guest. All he had left was his benevolence" (p. 65). The story exemplifies Wain's ability for capturing the essence of a personality through description and dialogue that we saw in *A Winter in the Hills*.

The fourth story, "A Message from the Pig-Man," sounds again the imaginative terrors within a child's mind. To understand the past, one may also recall the adventures of childhood, especially

the crucial period of adolescence when the child grows out of
innocence; often experiences pain, embarrassment, and disillusionment, but invariably acquires new knowledge, dignity, and
awareness of self. "Rafferty," on the other hand, reminds us of a
Hemingway story with its objective point of view and heavy
reliance on dialogue. The story ends with, " 'life's so full of
unexpected things, it pays to cultivate a taste for them' "
(p. 90)—as the young man goes on his way, leaving a girl who
took too long to make up her mind.

One of the most powerful stories in this collection is "Nuncle."
Tom Rogers is a drunken, once-famous novelist who decides he
must get married. He has not written for twenty years, but he is
certain that marriage to a steady, decent girl will set him to work
again. Daphne delights Tom when she not only accepts his
suggestion of marriage but proposes that they live with her
father, a retired businessman, in a roomy cottage in the depths of
the country. Tom, of course, finds he can no longer write; but his
father-in-law, an admirably conceived character, soon finds that
he can. So they agree that the former businessman will write the
great works and the former author will sell them under his
famous name. As for Daphne, she will do the typing. The
remainder of the story is a study of the inevitable problem: will
the reversal of roles damage the characters of the two men, and
to which of them will Daphne feel she is really married? For a
woman's allegiance is to the struggling genius, who needs her,
not to the man who is just out to sell things for money.

Of the stories in this collection, Wain is certainly at his best in
"Nuncle." It is a slower, more controlled piece in which subtle
irony and the hidden, destructive urges of his characters are
savored by both author and reader. Looking over the collection,
one critic compared the stories to Wain's novels with the
following results:

[Wain's] novels . . . have an immediacy, a bitter humour and a sure
touch. His disgust with the human condition as he finds it in his part of
contemporary England is very much in his parade of nasty parents,
loathsome children, caddish men and faithless women. But there are
redeeming qualities to balance this lop-sided vision. The more positive
elements, ruthless honesty, clever irony and vigor are present in good
measure in this his first collection of short stories, but here he gives us a
much deeper and more complex picture of disturbing and disturbed

children, and a more sympathetic insight into the lot of his wasted or burnt-out adults. Here too he is master of the paradoxical *bon mot* and of exaggerated invective.[6]

In the development of his novels, Wain showed an increase in stature and compassion; he became less angry, more thoughtful. This same quality comes to the fore in his next collection, *Death of the Hind Legs and Other Stories.* In "King Caliban," for example, Wain relates the destruction of a simple and loving wrestler whose innocence is manipulated by his wife and brother. In its humorous development, the tale recalls the element of exaggeration in Mark Twain's tall tales. A more substantial piece, "Come In, Captain Grindle," combines poignancy with suspense. It opens upon a young housewife, Laura Daniel, who suspects that her husband is unfaithful yet lacks the courage to follow up on her suspicions. The tale ends on a note often found in Wain's writing: "Turning on her side, she stared with wide motionless eyes at her approaching loneliness."[7]

Loneliness is again the theme of "A Visit at Tea-Time," a study of the regressive yearnings of a man confronting his boyhood home and garden. Implicit in this story is Wain's by now familiar moral position that the modern world is often cold and amoral, and that the only true value is to be found in the tradition of the past. Here the author of this sad tale makes his point with sufficient emphasis:

The room, however, had changed almost out of recognition. The furniture was modern, with that dead, unreverberating modernity that seems to belong to the laboratory and the machine-shop, never to humanity. . . . *Something* must have caused this bright, dead overlay of up-to-dateness, this combination of bright colours which only succeeded in conveying a hopeless inner drabness. (p. 50)

Wain also shows particular compassion for the youngster in "Manhood," in which a boy is forced into a rigid athletic program by his father. This time, Wain seems to be saying, imagination, pitted against the harsh realities of the world, triumphs, even though that triumph is more than any adult, in the circumstances, would have dared to expect. Wain's dramatic powers are illustrated again in "Darkness," the story of a frightened man's journey through the blackness of a Spanish village. Wain effectively captures the urgency of the man's panic, so that his relief and gratitude emerge at the end with contrasting force. The pathos generated by the appearance of a kindly blind man who leads him to daylight is conveyed with depth, too.

On a lighter note, love between generations is the theme in "The Valentine Generation." Again narrated in the first person, a mail collector argues life and love with a young girl anxious to retrieve a letter to her boyfriend that she had dropped into the mailbox too impulsively. Love, she says, is " 'wanting to be with somebody all the time' " (p. 91), and the mailman agrees.

Two other stories are heavily ironic. "Further Education" concerns a cynical tycoon who renews acquaintances with a couple he knew during his Oxford undergraduate days, only to cuckold the idealistic husband as he had done twenty years before. Understatement and characterization through dialogue distinguish this story. Rather more considerable for its social statement is "Down Our Way," which exposes another kind of ruthlessness—the ruthlessness of racial prejudice. A suburban family with a room to rent is extra nice to an Indian, thinking he is actually a reporter in disguise. When they learn that they have rented the room to a *real* Indian, their self-righteous respectability comes to a head.

Nostalgia is the tone of "Goodnight, Old Daisy." Wain follows old Mr. Williams to a museum in which is stored the train he once operated. His thoughts tell of the symbolic identification so essential to his peace of mind. In his death at the end is a hint of the tragic fatuity of his mechanical obsession. Here, as in "The Valentine Generation," Wain makes explicit his feelings of past tradition when he writes that "the world had gone. It had shrunk, and become flat and grey and washed-out" (p. 136). From the cab of the engine, "the world looked sane and comely" (p. 136). In his next story, "Giles and Penelope," Penelope recognizes that she and the common prostitute are not far apart. And the title story, "Death of the Hind Legs," concerns a tacky pantomime troupe playing its last show at a condemned theater. A valiant old professional, serving as hindquarters of a makebelieve horse, dies on stage. Like others of Wain's stories, "Death of the Hind Legs" takes a bizarre theme but treats it with kindliness and hope rather than with satire.

Looking back over this collection, we find that the stories are balanced in content and form, tone and skill. Most notable is the range of plots and variety of points of view. The theme is that a search for one's origins or for the glories of a lost youth brings the past into the present and aids the understanding of the present. In all, sympathy, gentle humor, and understanding mark the Wain treatment of his people.

As one commentator noted, the stories in the third collection, entitled *The Life Guard and Other Stories*, highlight some of Wain's favorite preoccupations:

with people pushing themselves to the limits of their moral and physical strength, with problems of adjustment after a crisis, with the social and intellectual rat-race in a territory where literature, journalism, sex and money combine to an odd confrontation in the thicket of the human jungle.[8]

In each of the first three stories, a man is challenged by death. The title story focuses on a life guard who loves the water and hopes to be near it forever. His life-guarding at the local British resort seems to assure it and may even set the struggling Red Rocks on the road to success. Eager to show how safe for swimming the ocean is under his watchful eye, he sets up a demonstration emergency in which a friend is to stage a fake drowning. Unfortunately, events get the better of him and he really drowns. The life guard meets the challenge of death with broken resignation as he realizes that he will have to leave the town and the sea. "It is a complete story, exciting, subtle, and resolved—resolved in a resounding dilemma."[9]

The narrator in "While the Sun Shines" also faces the challenge of death, but under different circumstances. He is a tractor driver who must drive over a treacherous hill where a predecessor has been maimed. In doing so, he conquers the field, his own fears, his boss (who wanted him fired if he refused), and the boss's wife in the process. The narrator's moral victory goes beyond physical victory; he meets the challenge of death with sexual power.

Certainly the most disturbing story in the collection is "The Innocent," in which Wain depicts a sedate family car as a place of nameless forebodings. A family man on the verge of a breakdown drives over a badger in the dark. He conquers his own fears of the dark and releases the mystery of death by insisting on burying the badger by flashlight.

Each of the above stories is a serious exploration of a moment of moral crisis or self-knowledge. There follow two lighter entertainment pieces. One, entitled "I Love You, Ricky," concerns two teenage girls who adore the same pop singer and organize their lives around a cuff link from his shirt. The other tale is "You Could Have Fooled Me," an account of a girl doing artistic modeling. She is hired by an artist who intends to cover her with paint and roll her on the canvas.

The final story in the collection is an excellent example of Wain's ability to use a notable incident to illuminate some aspect of character. "A Man in a Million" is narrated by a literary journalist. It is a portrait of Lovelace, a misfit, whose life is a string of turning points that lead to nowhere except to the next improbable role. Wain's observant eye catches the absurdity of the roleplayer, watching as Lovelace becomes a rich woman's plaything and a professional militant, without abandoning his lack of moral principle.

What can be drawn from this survey of Wain's short stories? We cannot fail to notice the similarities between them and his longer fiction. For one thing, they share the same outlook on life: like his early novels, many of his stories reveal Wain to be a comic with a fundamental seriousness. As an acute observer, he chooses to laugh at distasteful and ridiculous things in modern life. What is more, both genres present us a wealth of situations, characters, and points of view through which Wain artistically examines the problems of the individual's relation to society, enriches our scope of acquaintance with fictional persons, and, more specifically, further defines his vision of the world. And his judgment of the reality he sees is often severe: in it, art and imagination have been replaced by journalism, people by the machine, love by sex, folklore by popular movies, work by productivity, and villages by suburbs.

It is also evident that most of the time Wain is interested in ordinary life, interior and exterior, and not in the fantastic or surreal. Wain manages to project a special concern for the things which personally concern most people living in the modern world. The world of his fiction is a world to which most readers can readily respond. In all, "he manages to remain himself and to convey the same sense of integrity that distinguishes his novels."[10] Of Wain himself, it seems perfectly sound to predict that his reputation will ultimately rest upon his novels *and* his short stories.

II *The Poetry*

This study is limited to a consideration of Wain's accomplishments as a writer of prose, for it is primarily in this capacity that he has gained prominence in British literature. He has published eight volumes of poetry, however: *Mixed Feelings* (1951), his first important creative work, published in a limited edition of 120 copies and dedicated to Kingsley Amis; *A Word Carved on a Sill* (1956); *Weep Before God: Poems* (1961); *Wildtrack: A Poem* (1965); *Letters to Five Artists* (1969); *The Shape of Feng* (1972); *Feng: A Poem* (1975) and *Poems: 1949–1979* (1980). Various poems in the collections should be considered, some because of the light which they throw upon his fiction, others because they are good in their own right. Furthermore, the writing of poetry is for Wain far from being an ancillary activity to the writing of prose. In commenting on his literary career, he has observed, "My poems, which are the best things I have done, are naturally unknown because this is not a poetry-reading age."[11]

About the time Wain debuted as a novelist, the BBC hired him to succeed John Lehmann as editor of "First Readings"—a weekly radio program which introduced promising young writers to the public. Because he was exposed to a vast amount of writing from many contributors, Wain developed an idea of what was happening to the mind of the age. He now feels this exposure helped to make him a better literary journalist. Moreover, he found himself with the opportunity to introduce new writers whose views he shared. These writers included Kingsley Amis, A. Alvarez, D. J. Enright, and Philip Larkin, all of whom wrote both poetry and fiction.

In 1956 an anthology called *New Lines* brought many of these British poets to wider attention. A distinctive feature of their verse was a rejection of the passion and romantic rhetoric of Dylan Thomas—whose voice dominated the early part of the decade. Instead, they paid greater attention to structure and drew their subjects and language from everyday life. Because of these similarities in content and form, the poets came to be known among literary journalists as "The Movement." The poets saw their writing as an alternative to the symbolic and allusive poetry of T. S. Eliot and his followers. In a movement away from allusion, obscurity, and excess of style, the poets encouraged precision, lucidity, and craftsmanship. They concentrated on honesty of thought and feeling to project a "businesslike intention to communicate with the reader."[12] Although not all of them were practicing critics, without exception they brought "a critical consciousness to the writing of their poems."[13] Of Wain's early poems we may say that he does not preach, he avoids the emotion of Dylan Thomas, and he, like the other Movement poets, respects Philip Larkin as the voice of the "group."

Wain's novels match closely the general attitudes attributed to the Movement writers. Like his early verse, for example, Wain's deceptively simple novels have been written with the same criteria he imposed on his poetry; thus, they must be looked at with a kind of standard applicable in the nineteenth century. It will not do to read his novels with a measure suitable only to Joyce and Faulkner. Rather, Wain's intellectual and literary ancestors antedate the great modernist writers, and they have helped to shape him into a kind of nineteenth-century clergyman: a literate man of good will who seeks to instruct people of some intelligence. Thus, his early verse—in *Mixed Feelings*—and his first few novels—through *The Contenders*—may be appreciated for their common-sense approach. He writes clearly. He avoids extremes or excessive stylistic experimentation. He is witty, satirical, and didactic with a moral dignity often crossed by faint touches of metaphysical wit.

With each succeeding volume of verse, Wain has advanced his range and technique. Some of the poems in *A Word Carved on a Sill*—"Poem Feigned to have been Written by an Electronic Brain," for example—reveal "a journalistic immediacy and wit and a movement toward the public poem."[14] In "The Bad Thing," he achieves a study of depressive states similar to *The Smaller Sky*. Wain's development continues in his next collection, *Weep Before God*, in which the poems are looser, more declamatory than the verse in the earlier volumes. For this reason and others, critics considered it to be one of Wain's most impressive collections. Commentators found a more adventurous range and rhythm in "Poem Without a Main Verb" (a riddling poem), "Anniversary" (an autobiographical reflection), and "Brooklyn

Heights" (a topographical meditation).[15] And he is direct and unsentimental in "Anecdote of 2 a.m." when he says:

> I could not tell what dreams disturbed her heart.
> She spoke, and never knew my tongue was tied.
> I longed to bless her but she lay apart.[16]

In "A Song about Major Eatherly" his poetry is more public as he ponders the troubled later career of an American pilot involved in the nuclear attack on Japan in 1945. In "A Boisterous Poem About Poetry," Wain's concern with the inhumanity of science— the mechanical and industrial—is seen when he says: "Metal hates flesh, / Hates everything that has a beating heart" (VI, 5-6). From this man-hating material we make our man-hating machines:

> On the surface they flatter our intelligence,
> They are all smiles, they bend to our tasks:
> Then suddenly they turn and savage us. (VI, 15-17)

Since *Weep Before God*, Wain has developed powerfully in the direction of politics and social commentary. What separates him from his contemporaries is his eighteenth-century manner in diction and his moral dignity. The later poems embody, in a more compact form, many of the feelings and attitudes which are expressed in his novels; frequently, in fact, they have to do with the institutions and prejudices of society in a satirical manner. As we saw in his novels, Wain is concerned chiefly with human efforts to seek happiness and self-fulfillment. The search for happiness and "human independence" is the subject of *Wildtrack*, a single long poem published in 1965. We find here a considerable variety of meter, including terza rima, a free sestina, a sonnet, and mock dance-lyric, as Wain passes freely from the past to the present.

In 1969 Wain published *Letters to Five Artists*. He states in the preface that, with one exception, the five poems were written not only to stand by themselves but also "to take on another dimension when read together and seen as one larger work."[17] He also mentions that he can never see human life "except as an inextricable scrambling of private and public" (p. 9). Hence, the theme of this volume is the theme of *Wildtrack*, with "its inward-looking Night-self and outward-looking Day-self that together constitute the human personality" (p. 9). The basic rhythm of the poems is iambic pentameter, thus showing the influence of serious English poetry, and the poems are directed at some acquaintances who inspired him. Each of the five artists—Victor Neep (painter), Elizabeth Jennings and Anthony Conran (poets), Lee Lubbers, S.J. (sculptor), and Bill Coleman (jazz trumpeter)—is not only a personal friend of Wain's but also a visionary whose imagination presents to the world a light that guides the poet and the reader toward recognition—of himself, of the artists, and of the world.

In one of his more recent collections—*Feng: A Poem* (1975)— Wain worked to set the sequence of poems in northern Europe during the early Middle Ages; however, the "reality they explore is equally that of our own time and place."[18] In a prefatory note, the author explains that the design of the work comes from the *Historia Danica* of Saxo Grammaticus—from which Shakespeare borrowed the plot for his own *Hamlet*. In the original story, Horwendil, father of Amleth, kills the King of Norway in single combat. Feng, his brother, poisons him and marries Gerutha, his queen. Amleth assumes madness out of which Feng tries but fails to trick him by means of a beautiful woman. The prince voyages to England, returns to kill Feng, and settles down to an active reign.

Unlike Shakespeare, who concentrates on the character of Amleth, Wain focuses on Feng—"the sick and hallucinated [*sic*] person who seizes power and then has to live with it" (p. iv)—and the contrast of natural innocence and human depravity. Wain comments:

Since I have lived through an age in which raving madmen have had control of great and powerful nations, the theme naturally seems to me an important one. (p. iv)

From what has been said of the themes of some of Wain's poems, it can be seen that there are parallels between his verse and fiction. Much of his poetic artistry rests in his ability to concretize—through personality and theme—many of the questions which have perplexed man almost since his beginning but which in modern times have become the province principally of academicians. In this he resembles Philip Larkin. Because Wain's poetry reflects his determination to speak to a wider range of readers than many of his modernist predecessors, it reflects, too, his faith in the common reader to recognize and respond to traditional philosophical concerns.. These concerns include his sense of the dignity of human beings in the midst of an oftentimes cruel, indifferent, cynical world. His concern is with a world caught up in time, desire, and disappointment.

III *The Critic*

In approaching John Wain as a literary critic, the first thing to grasp is that literary criticism is, to Wain, a "useful" art.[19] The critic is out to persuade and to influence others. At its best, criticism preserves a sense of the past against which the present may be measured. Wain further defines the art as "the discussion, between equals, of works of literature, with a view to establishing common ground on which judgements of value can be based" (p. 187). The title "critic," he asserts, is that which must be earned by one who is prepared to put himself through a rather vigorous, long training period. Wain's own academic background accounts in part for the solidity of his accomplishments: he is well informed about literature and writes within its established tradition. Because he is a novelist and poet, Wain has the advantage of discussing literature as a fellow craftsman. James Gindin[20] has commented that Wain analyzes and explains what he sees clearly and cogently. We always know what Wain is saying: his descriptions of books are clear and his criteria are intelligible. In both his criticism and his fiction, therefore, we find that his observations are accurate and meaningful, and that his perceptions are intelligently explored and demonstrated.

Moreover, like everyone who reads seriously, Wain has sometimes turned for help to other critics. He attributes part of his success as a writer to four individuals: his tutor, C. S. Lewis; Samuel Johnson; William Empson; and Edmund Wilson. Were we to ask what these four men have in common, Wain would reply that

they are all both inward-looking—concerned with language, sensitive to the ingredients that go to make a literary effect—and outward-looking; they all value literature as a source of aesthetic pleasure and emotional satisfaction, but even more for its involvement in the world, what it can tell us about ourselves and one another, what it can do for us in helping us to live our own lives.[21]

Like these four critics, Wain has "the same root, language; the same trunk, a strong individual personality; and the same branches, spreading out into wide political and social issues."[22]

Also central to Wain's critical stance is his belief that, in order to judge the quality of a piece of literature, the critic must make a moral as well as an imaginative judgment. In "Along the Tightrope," his contribution to *Declaration*, we are reminded of one of Shakespeare's purposes in writing *Hamlet* when Wain says:

The artist's function is always to *humanize* the society he is living in, to assert the importance of humanity in the teeth of whatever is currently trying to annihilate that importance.[23]

Yet the moral standards a critic applies cannot be so narrow that they contradict general human experience, and his emotions cannot be so personally involved that he sees art merely as personal wish-fulfillment. Criticism that is narrow in scope is not seeking literary truth but rather the satisfaction of a prior appetite. Hence, running through Wain's criticism is one central thread: the directness with which he relates literature to life, and the consequential distrust with which he views all writing that goes to work obliquely, by means of symbolism or the integral use of figurative language. Like his fiction, his critical essays and reviews are written not for an exclusive, erudite clique, but for as broad a class of reasonably intelligent, but not necessarily scholarly, readers as possible. If his essays' unpretentious, relaxed manner keeps them from constituting what the world likes to call a "significant body of critical thought," they are nevertheless well worth reading, full of vitality and insight, putting us in contact with a Wain who is every bit as real as the one he exploits in his fiction and verse.

IV   *Criticism and Miscellaneous Essays*

The scope of Wain's first collection, *Preliminary Essays* (1957), exposes us at once to the extraordinary range of his literary interests. Restoration comedy, Ovid, Wordsworth, Tennyson, Browning, Hopkins, Housman, Bennett, and modern poetry—all are embraced by a sensibility whose interests are primarily those of the popular reader he extols. This is the reader who comes to a book looking for insight into the way people act, think, and feel, who is eager to experience someone else's imaginative attempt to make sense of the world.

The preface establishes the tone and the guiding critical concerns of the entire book. Wain explains that the book is called "preliminary" because it is the record of part of an apprenticeship: "it takes a long time to learn to become a critic, and I have only been at it for ten years" (p. x). Typical of his generation of writers, Wain's tone is direct, relaxed, conversational, as he asks of literature those rather primitive questions that intelligent readers have always asked: Are the emotions honest? Is the work unified? And above all, is the vision of life embedded in the work of art coherent and substantial, shaping our own perceptions of things in significant ways? These questions speak to the moral and intellectual tradition of English Puritanism.

Of the essays, "The Quality of Arnold Bennett" is perhaps the best-known instance of Wain's talent for discussing writers whose work has a bearing on the writings of his own generation. In this well-balanced essay, Wain asserts that Bennett has been undervalued. He places the writer in the tradition of Daniel Defoe—Wain's own fiction owes something to the Defoe line— and justifies *The Old Wives' Tale* when he says:

The right kind of reader can extract a rich poetic experience from the heaviest and most matter-of-fact compilation, *so long as it is honest;* in fact it is easier to respond richly to this kind than to the over-lush imaginative novel that provides your poetry for you. (p. 155)

The pleasantly accessible surface of Wain's fiction with its clear linear chronology and its wealth of social observations is similar to something Bennett might have given us.

Most critics found his next collection, *Essays on Literature and Ideas* (1963), to be disappointing. Wain's motives for writing the essays, he claims, are those of John Middleton Murray's confession that as he grew older he came to feel the truth that criticism records the adventures of one's soul among masterpieces. This is the kind of pleasure Wain finds in writing his own criticism.

A House for the Truth (1972), on the other hand, has proven to be one of his most popular and successful collections. Many of his commitments reflected in his fiction come through clearly in this book. Perhaps the chief of these is his common-sense insistence on clarity itself. His standard is "convincingness"—practical and businesslike in approach. While he does not regard himself as a great critic, Wain hastens to add he does believe that "in this throw-away age, the notion of building something as solid as a house seems . . . true and salutary."[24]

It should come as no surprise to us that Wain singles out George Orwell, Samuel Johnson, and Pasternak as his "moral heroes," in the Carlylean sense. In his essays on these three writers, together with Flann O'Brien, Wain argues from the point of view of a moralist. Although he says he is still far from having worked out a "common ground on which judgements of value can be based" (p. 2), his own governing principle is clear: he believes firmly in the abiding virtues of heroic individualism and integrity. He finds these virtues in the writers he discusses, and what is more, he tells us about their works with the enthusiasm and the detail of a craftsman rejoicing in the way it was done and wanting to share their pleasure. Moreover, his familiar attitude toward the contemporary literary scene is expressed in two additional essays, "A Salute to the Makers" and "The Vanishing Critic." In the former, Wain examines the effect of "know nothing populism" on the craft of poetry; in the latter, he perceives the critical office as becoming indolent in an age of throwaway literature.

Consistent with his views on criticism and the novel as expressed in *A House for the Truth* are his comments on the nature of poetry and the obligations of the poet in his next collection, *Professing Poetry* (1978). The nine lectures in this book were given in the first three years of Wain's five-year term as professor of poetry at Oxford (1973–1978). All nine lectures are linked together with a commentary intended to convey "the unique nature of the Oxford chair [and] the special atmosphere that surrounds it."[25] Included also is an appendix of poems he wrote during that five-year period.

Wain's announced purpose is twofold: to denounce those contemporary poets who have abandoned what Wain sees as essential parts of the English poetic tradition and whom he identifies with left-wing political protesters; and to praise those twentieth-century poets who have maintained the antimodernism tradition: Edward Thomas, the younger Auden, William Empson, and Philip Larkin.

"Let me be specific," he says. "The years since 1960 have seen a mass turning-away from the notion of poetry as an art that used to have something in common with music, and towards a more or less improvisatory style which aims at one of two objectives: either to simulate the ravings of a drug-addict, or to inculcate very simple political and social messages. In either case it represents the deliquescence of a tradition" (p. 38). Further on he complains about the decadence of contemporary verse, and says: "Form, which used to hold the precious liquor of a poem as a jug holds milk, is broken for no other purpose than to allow the milk to spill on to the ground. Verbal nuance and literary allusion are rejected as 'élitist,' the implied directive being that what all cannot achieve no one must. . . . Form is communication. It is a system of signals between writer and reader" (p. 38). Thus he reminds us that true poems originate in the most personal feelings of their authors and touch the most personal feelings of their readers.

Having seen how Wain deplores pointless or conspicuous technique, we can understand not only many of his practices as a poet, but his special admiration for writers like Edward Thomas, the early Auden, Empson, and Larkin, in whom technique is notably inconspicuous. Wain's emphasis here, as usual, is on the poet's obligation to the reader: to move and to please, perhaps to amuse, but never to ignore.

Of all of Wain's nonfiction, however, varying from autobiography to biography to literary criticism, many readers believe *Samuel Johnson* to be his best and most lasting work. In this monumental biography, many of Wain's commitments reflected in his other writings come through clearly and forcefully.

V Samuel Johnson

When Wain's biography of Samuel Johnson was published in 1974, Wain's stature as a scholar-artist arrived. Donald Greene and Angus Wilson, among other notables, showered it with praise; the Book-of-the-Month Club selected it as a feature of the month; and he received the James Tait Black Memorial Book Prize and the Whitbread Award—all this within four months.

How Wain came to write the biography is interesting indeed.

"Nobody can write the life of a man," wrote Johnson, "but those who have eaten and drunk and lived in social intercourse with him." By his reading and thinking, Wain has come as close to that as possible. Over the past thirty years he has read Johnson's *Lives of the Poets* every year, never failing "to find interest, instruction, amusement, somewhere in their pages."[26] Like Johnson, he has published several volumes of literary criticism and poetry, and he challenges us to consider him as a twentieth-century version of Johnson. We have learned already that Wain sees Johnson's life from the inside: he himself was born in the same district and social milieu, went to the same university, and has made his living in Grub Street. And we have seen how his love for the subject grew during his undergraduate years at Oxford. But there is more to the story.

In 1958 the American scholar Edmund Wilson presented Wain with a large, ledgerlike manuscript book. " 'It was a lovely book with green-tinted pages, easy on the eye.' "[27] Wain treasured it; he made part of it into an alphabetical section and divided another part into the years of Johnson's life. From 1958 on, Wain continued to make notes about people, places, and events in Johnson's life and his own unanswered questions about them. His work over these years is somewhat akin to Johnson's years laboring over the *Dictionary*. Then, in 1969, " 'the time just happened to come. I was between novels and between this and that and I said, let's do it now.' "[28] After months of reading — much of it in Oxford's Bodleian Library, where Dr. Johnson had also worked — Wain managed to fill in the gaps and to answer the questions. In 1972 he began writing *Samuel Johnson*. It was published two years later.

Wain was attracted to the idea for several reasons: not only would it give him an opportunity to express his admiration for the man, but more important, it offered a new formal challenge. Commenting on Boswell's *Life*, he said that although it is a great masterpiece, " 'his approach is that of the theater. You go from one scene to the next with a few sentences of narrative in between. It's brilliantly done, but narrative it isn't.' "[29] As we might expect, Wain called upon his talents as a novelist and dramatist to give a detailed account of Johnson's life. Because of his years of experience writing novels, Wain knew how to write narrative. " 'Boswell could not write narrative — thank God. He left something for us to do.' "[30]

Also, Wain begins his biography with the premise that Johnson has not yet been accorded his rightful reputation. He believes that Johnson, for the most part, is thought of as a "stupid old reactionary," rather than as a deeply humanitarian man who felt compassion for the "poor and outcast" (pp. 13, 14). For the origins of this distorted picture, Wain cites both Boswell's sentimental-romantic Toryism and Johnsonian scholars' tendency to write for each other rather than to a broader public. Wain's goal, therefore, is to present a picture of Johnson "as he actually was instead of as he is thought of" (p. 14).

Samuel Johnson, Wain asserts, is a popular biography "addressed to the intelligent general reader" (p. 13). He does not claim to come up with new material or explanations. Moreover, he avoided reading modern studies of Johnson while writing it because he preferred to draw his impressions directly from eighteenth-century sources. Some critics have taken Wain to task for not acknowledging his sources more directly; without footnotes, they said, differences of scholarly opinion and dependencies upon other works are hidden from all but the specialists. Others pointed out that the volume is a substantial work of synthesis of modern material and established sources. But as Wain explains in his preface, the scholar has been adequately catered to; this book is for the popular reader.

Samuel Johnson is both an account of Johnson—his life, times, and works—and an implicit statement of Wain's own views on the state of twentieth-century England. In its straightforward chronological structure, the book reminds us of a novel. It comprises thirty chapters divided among six main parts, each a major epoch of Dr. Johnson's life: In the Midlands; Grub Street; The Dictionary Years; "True, Evident and Actual Wisdom" (the years of Johnson as legendary conversationalist); Turtle and Burgundy (Johnson's comfortable years with Hester Thrale); An Honourable Peace. Thus Wain covers all the great moments of Johnson's career.

Beginning with a full portrait of Johnson's early life in Lichfield, Wain establishes the thematic threads which will run through the book. Here we see his monumental intellectual energy, his deeply passionate nature, his poverty, and his career defeats. Here also we have explained to us Johnson's life-long agony of guilt, attributed to his implacable mother. We learn that poverty compelled him to leave Oxford without a degree. We see him fail in his efforts first as a school usher then as a school proprietor-teacher, only to be hired to write for the *Gentleman's Magazine*. This latest development inspired him to move to London, where he emerged into English literary life. There, in Grub Street, he talked and wrote, researched, attacked the Whig hegemony, defended the Tory posture, and lived out his life.

In London Johnson met and married Tetty, but this union brought only temporary happiness. With pressure mounting to support himself and his wife, he became a parliamentary reporter. Then he thought of preparing an edition of Shakespeare. When this proposal was frustrated, he turned to the preparation of a dictionary of the English language. A number of wealthy Englishmen supported this project, and for a time he was content. In later years Johnson turned to Boswell and Hester Thrale for companionship. All along, Wain recounts Johnson's diseases of the body and torments of the soul.

The above summary gives some indication of how Wain uses his novelist's art to maintain the sense of the long passage of life. In addition to narrative pressure, Wain's sense of Johnson is strong, vivid, and original. He gives many illustrations of Johnson's talk which, "like his writing, is based on strong, vivid, concrete detail" (p. 249). Also, Wain's vivid descriptive powers give us a physical portrait of Johnson—with his huge limbs and weight, his awkwardness and ugliness, and his gross appetite and angers. For instance: "huge bones not yet adequately covered in flesh, wild staring eyes, scrofula-scarred face" (p. 33); his "terrific mule-kick at Chesterfield" (p. 177); "like the heroic caryatid that he was" (p. 287). Thus, a principal factor behind the power of *Samuel Johnson* is Wain's use of images and concrete details. Restricting himself generally to the narrative of Johnson's life (though interludes of analysis and interpretation do occur), Wain succeeds in bringing Johnson before us in all his power, versatility, and passion.

Wain's sense of milieu is powerful, also. We see the England of 1728, through which Johnson rode to Oxford; the London of a decade later, when the child of the provinces finally faced the metropolis; or the Lichfield market on the September afternoon of Johnson's birth:

Wednesday, 18 September 1709: the market Square in Lichfield was quiet, for this was not a trading day. The occasional rattle of a cart, or the talk and laughter of a knot of citizens passing the time of day at a corner, would sound clear across the square, while at regular intervals the long swell of melody from the great cathedral bells came washing over the rooftops. All these sounds penetrated to the ears of Sarah Johnson, the bookseller's wife, as she lay in her bedroom in the handsome three-storied house that dominated the north-eastern end of the square. (p. 17)

Here is the novelist at work. Wain's picturesque detail, his vivid sense of the social and geographical context, are all obvious. He writes easily and unaffectedly. His style is even, with a sobriety of tone. His prose is plain and strong.

There are occasional lapses in tone, however, some of which commentators found to be symptomatic of a certain frivolity. For example: Johnson was "plugging himself in to" (p. 29) Renaissance thought; in the dark days of the 1740s "help was at hand. The United States Cavalry was just over the next hill, in the shape of a posse of booksellers" (p. 129); or, "Then Fate, as so often at this period of Johnson's life, dealt from the bottom of the deck" (p. 57). But these lapses certainly do not obscure the very real virtues of the book. In its sympathy and intelligence, it is a splendid testament to Johnson. His originality, his goodness, his ability to experience the pure delight of people, art, and life are all captured by Wain. But there is more.

Of particular importance to us is Wain as moralizer. He tries to make Johnson relevant to modern life and repeatedly uses him as a means of commenting on literary and intellectual standards in the contemporary world. Wain's recurrent interpretive comments reveal a conservative feeling. He characterizes eighteenth-century England, and he stresses its difference from the twentieth century by noting its stability. For example, on the subject of Johnson's trust in reason:

An age that puts its trust in the ordering intellect will distrust and underplay the instincts. An age like ours which worships the instinctual will become anti-rational. It is no accident that our age has seen reason and lucidity sink to their lowest level of esteem since man came down from the trees. (p. 157)

Elsewhere Wain comments, "In his day there was probably no such thing as an ugly house, table, stool or chair in the whole kingdom" (p. 43). At one point, after dramatizing Johnson in conversation, Wain says:

Of such stuff, it seems, was the dinner-table conversation made, in the literary London of those days; we, who live among the scorched and blackened ruins, can only hope to imagine what such talk must have been like. (p. 202)

Although such moralisms interrupt the continuity of the narrative, they should not surprise us. We have already seen how, in his other criticism and fiction, Wain has affirmed many of the values held by Johnson. These include his faith in reason, the validity of art as the touchstone of civilization, and the value and relevance of the past. From the biography, it is clear that Wain sees eighteenth-century provincial life as a time of dignity, pride, and self-sufficiency lacking in the twentieth century. Like Johnson, he defends the value of reason and moderation, common sense, moral courage, and intellectual self-respect.

It is obvious that Wain holds a loving esteem for the man and his work. His biography is written with sympathy for his agonies, with awe for his intellect, and with admiration for his stoicism. Wain is personally involved—it is written out of a lifetime interest in Johnson—and there is perhaps no finer way to praise the book than to say it makes us feel for Johnson what Wain and all admirers feel for him. I cannot improve upon Christopher Ricks's judgment when he wrote:

Among the many achievements of John Wain's vividly humane life of Johnson is that it does justice to the range and depth of this just and merciful man. His dignity, his unexpected gentleness; his literary triumphs as a poet, critic, dictionary-maker, editor, essayist, and as a one-man university uniting the best of faculties; his courage in the face of sickness, melancholia and even madness: all of these are alive in Mr. Wain's firm and delicate pages. It is a noble story nobly told.[31]

CHAPTER 7

In Retrospect

WHAT sort of conclusions does this examination of John Wain's work suggest? Most readily apparent is his versatility, manifesting itself in the wide range of subjects in fiction and nonfiction. A complete man of letters, he has turned out novels and short stories, poetry, drama, as well as countless articles on literature and literary criticism. His continuing impact on the literary scene is attested to by extensive publications of both hardcover re-editions and original works.

Although Wain continues to show much promise as a writer, some scholars feel he has fallen short of expectations. Those who dislike his work find him to be repetitious, hasty, and sentimental, whereas those who praise him do so for his elaborate plotting, sincerity, and wit. Some commentators conclude that Wain takes his critical writings too seriously and his novel-writing not seriously enough. In spite of this judgment, his principal strength continues to be his engagement with serious, important ideas. In all three genres his vigor and his sincerity mark him as a member of the distinguished company of scholar-artists.

Wain is clearly an accomplished novelist. In the tradition of the eighteenth-century novel, he fulfills most effectively the novelist's basic task of telling a good story. The techniques of modern novelists—placing biased and implicated characters close to the center of action in order to make for complexity of perspective, foreshortening of plot to allow for dramatic concentration, and jumbling narrative sequences to involve the reader in a struggle for the meaning of events—do not figure in Wain's books. They move along at an even pace; he avoids stylistic experimentation and relies upon a simple, tightly constructed, and straightforward plot; clarity; good and bad characters; and a controlled point of view. We need only think of

Joyce, Kafka, and Eliot, and the contrast is clear. What many of his novels ask from us is not some feat of analysis, but a considered fullness of response, a readiness to assert to, even if not to agree with, his vision of defeat.

Wain also has the seriocomic touch. With varying success, Charles Lumley, Edgar Banks, Joe Shaw, and George Links are all creations of the comic spirit, characters who are cherished as samples of the immense variety of human behavior. But here as elsewhere Wain tries to be a balanced writer. There is a serious, almost tragic dimension even to these more lightly presented characters. And there are, of course, other characters in whom the tragic element dominates: Arthur Geary, for example, in *The Smaller Sky*, or the unhappy Giles Hermitage in *The Pardoner's Tale*.

If his methods of characterization are consistent, his success with his creations is not. In the early novels, for instance, the subject matter seems trivial at times, and only with difficulty do we summon that kind of involvement with character and situation which presses upon us in the best of Wain's work. In these early novels everything is controlled by Wain's personal vision of life; we feel the characters and events are allowed to stiffen into mere illustrations of ideas. In the later novels, by comparison, we find most remarkable the psychological verisimilitude: the majority of characters in *The Young Visitors, The Smaller Sky, A Winter in the Hills*, and *The Pardoner's Tale* are credible. Although we are still aware of the presence of a mind shaping the contours of the plot, we also sense that the author is allowing the characters a measure of autonomy and idiosyncratic existence.

Wain is also accomplished in his creation of place and atmosphere. In *Strike the Father Dead* he fully captures the grayness of a London day, the grayness of lives spent under its pall, the grayness of the people who wander its streets. When Wain describes an afternoon in which Giles Hermitage forces himself to work in the subdued light at home; when Arthur Geary walks the platforms at Paddington Station; when Charles Lumley walks in on a literary gathering; when Roger Furnivall makes his way home through the Welsh countryside—at such moments we encounter Wain's ability to develop and control the setting and atmosphere. Encompassing this ability is the memorable way in which the novels celebrate a central conviction of Wain. They affirm the significance of the seemingly commonplace life and of the seemingly commonplace man.

The themes communicated through Wain's criticism and novels are, like his method, consistent. It is clear that he sees the eighteenth century as a time of dignity, pride, and self-sufficiency—qualities lacking in the twentieth century. Like Samuel Johnson, Wain defends the value of reason, moderation, common sense, moral courage, and intellectual self-respect. Moreover, his fictional themes of the dignity of the human being, the difficulty of survival in the modern world, and the perils of success have established him principally as a moralist concerned with ethical issues. In later works, the value of tradition, the notion of human understanding, and the ability to love and suffer become the chief moral values. In all his novels, his own feelings are primarily concerned with the problem of defining the moral worth of the individual. For these reasons, Wain is recognized as a scholarly and poignant observer of the human scene.

One last word about Wain's capacities as a novelist. Clearly, the spiritual dimension is missing in the world he describes: God is, if not dead, absent. And yet there is frequently the hint or at least the possibility of renewal, which is the closest Wain comes to any sort of recognized affirmation. Charles Lumley, Joe Shaw, Jeremy Coleman, and Roger Furnivall are all characters who seem to be, by the end of their respective novels, on the verge of rebirth of a sort, on the threshold of reintegration and consequent regeneration. In each case, this renewal depends on the ability of the individual to come to terms with himself and his situation, to confront and accept at a stroke past, present, and future, and to accept and tolerate the contradictions inherent in all three.

Contradiction is where we started with Wain, and where we end. Above all, what he shows us in his fiction is the imponderable variegation of human experience, in an ultimately unjust world. Joy and sorrow intermingle, as do the lovely and the grotesque, sanity and dementia, love and lovelessness. Wain's vision is one of disenchantment with the values of modern life, and more deeply, it asserts the power of that "injustice which triumphs so flagrantly in the destinies of men." In allowing himself to respond so sensitively to the tragic aspects of the life which he sees around him, Wain is of course doing nothing new.

To Shakespeare, to Sophocles of old, and to the writer of the Book of Job, human misery was an old story. But his deep compassion for human suffering and tenderness for the unfortunate denote a sensibility more needed than ever in an age when violence, brutality, and cynicism are all too prevalent.

Notes and References

Preface

1. "Plain Man of Letters," *Nation* 185(October 26, 1957): 285.
2. "Talking Turkey," *New Statesman and Nation* 54(August 10, 1957): 179.
3. "Man of Letters—and Much More," *Wall Street Journal*, February 24, 1975, p. 11.

Chapter One

1. Richard Mayne, "Travelling Man," *New Statesman* 70(October 8, 1965): 528.
2. John Wain, "Introduction," in his *A House for the Truth: Critical Essays* (New York: Viking Press, 1973), p. 1.
3. "Introduction," in his *Samuel Johnson* (New York: Viking Press, 1975), p. 14.
4. *Professing Poetry* (London: Macmillan, 1977), p. 268.
5. *Sprightly Running* (New York: St. Martin's Press, 1963), p. 65. All subsequent page references in this chapter are to this edition.
6. *Professing Poetry*, p. 270.
7. Ibid.
8. Ibid.
9. Ibid., p. 157.
10. *Samuel Johnson*, p. 184.
11. Ibid.
12. "John Wain," in *The Writer's Place: Interviews on the Literary Situation in Contemporary Britain*, edited by Peter Firchow (Minneapolis: University of Minnesota Press, 1974), p. 320.
13. *Professing Poetry*, p. 9.
14. Willa F. Valencia, "The Picaresque Tradition in the Contemporary English and American Novel," Ph.D. dissertation, University of Illinois, 1968.
15. Kenneth Allsop, "The Neutralists," in his *The Angry Decade: A Survey of the Cultural Revolt of the Nineteen-Fifties* (London: Peter Owen, 1964), p. 51.
16. "Books of the Year—1," London *Sunday Times*, December 25, 1955, p. 4.

135

17. Elgin W. Mellown, "Steps Toward Vision: The Development of Technique in John Wain's First Seven Novels," *South Atlantic Quarterly* 17(Summer 1969): 330.

18. "Bi-Focus," London *Times*, September 5, 1969, p. 11.

19. "John Wain," p. 314.

Chapter Two

1. R. D. Charques, "New Novels," *Spectator* 191(October 2, 1953): 380.

2. London *Sunday Times*, October 5, 1953, p. 12.

3. "New Novels," *New Statesman and Nation*, 46(October 24, 1953): 496.

4. "Here, in a Manner of Speaking, Comes Tom Jones Again," *New York Herald Tribune Book Review*, March 21, 1954, p. 3.

5. Anon., "Briefly Noted," *New Yorker* 30(March 20, 1953): 114.

6. Norman Shrapnel, "New Fiction," *Manchester Guardian*, October 2, 1953, p. 4.

7. Anon., "Matters of Conscience," *Times Literary Supplement*, October 9, 1953, p. 641.

8. "The Unhappy Drifter," *New York Times Book Review*, March 21, 1954, p. 5.

9. "A bright first novel about a very bright young man," *Truth* 154(February 5, 1954): 185.

10. "A Sort of Rebels," in his *The Novel Now: A Guide to Contemporary Fiction* (New York: W. W. Norton, 1967), pp. 144, 146.

11. "Along the Tightrope," in *Declaration*, edited by Tom Maschler (New York: E. P. Dutton, 1958), p. 83.

12. Elgin W. Mellown, "Steps Toward Vision: The Development of Technique in John Wain's First Seven Novels," *South Atlantic Quarterly* 17(Summer 1969): 332.

13. *Hurry on Down* (New York: Viking Press, 1965), p. 33. All subsequent page references in this chapter, unless otherwise identified, are to this edition of the novel.

14. Mellown, p. 331.

15. "Introduction," in his *Hurry on Down* (London: Secker and Warburg, 1978), p. xiii.

16. *Living in the Present* (New York: G. P. Putnam's Sons, 1960), p. 249. All subsequent page references in this chapter, unless otherwise identified, are to this edition of the novel.

17. *Sprightly Running* (New York: St. Martin's Press, 1963), p. 170.

18. Michael Walzer, "John Wain: The Hero in Limbo," *Perspective* 10(Summer-Autumn 1958): 142.

19. G. S. Fraser, "The Novel in the 1950s," in his *The Modern Writer and His World* (Baltimore: Penguin Books, 1964), pp. 175, 176.

20. See, for example: S. W. Dawson, "A Personal Report on the

Literary Fifties," *Audit* 1(February 1960): i, 14; James Gindin, "The Reassertion of the Personal," *Texas Quarterly* 4(Fall 1958): 126-34; James W. Lee, "Introduction: VIII: John Wain," in his *John Braine*, Twayne English Authors Series, edited by Elizabeth A. Bowman (Boston: Twayne Publishers, 1968), pp. 26-30; William Van O'Connor, "John Wain: The Will to Write," *Wisconsin Studies in Contemporary Literature* 1(Winter 1960): 35-49; Colin Wilson, "The Writer and Publicity," *Encounter* 13(November 1959): 9.

21. "Along the Tightrope," p. 85.

22. *The Contenders* (New York: St. Martin's Press, 1958), p. 278. All subsequent page references in this chapter, unless otherwise identified, are to this edition of the novel.

23. "The Moral Center of John Wain's Fiction," in his *Postwar British Fiction: New Accents and Attitudes* (Berkeley and Los Angeles: University of California Press, 1962), p. 137.

24. *Chicago Sunday Tribune*, May 18, 1958, p. 2.

25. Mellown, p. 333.

26. "Top People," *Spectator* 198(March 28, 1958): 400.

27. "Rat Race to the Top," *New York Times Book Review*, April 27, 1958, p. 4.

28. "John Wain: The Will to Write," *Wisconsin Studies in Contemporary Literature* 1(Winter 1960): 46.

29. "John Wain Attacks Competitiveness in Our Society," New York *Herald Tribune Book Review*, April 27, 1958, p. 7.

30. Gindin, "The Moral Center of John Wain's Fiction," p. 135.

31. *A Travelling Woman* (New York: St. Martin's Press, 1959), p. 154. All subsequent page references in this chapter, unless otherwise identified, are to this edition of the novel.

32. Gindin, "The Moral Center of John Wain's Fiction," p. 136.

33. "John Wain and John Barth: The Angry and the Accurate," *Massachusetts Review* 1(May 1960): 585.

34. O'Connor, p. 48.

35. Mellown, p. 335.

36. O'Connor, p. 48.

37. "Various Formalities," *Spectator* 202(March 13, 1959): 380.

38. "An Oft-Told Tale," *Commonweal* 70(June 12, 1959): 309.

39. "Along the Tightrope," p. 86.

Chapter Three

1. *Sprightly Running* (New York: St. Martin's Press, 1963), p. 208.

2. Walter Allen, "Rebels and Ancestors in a War That Is Constantly Renewed," *New York Times Book Review*, September 23, 1962, p. 4.

3. Elgin W. Mellown, "Steps Toward Vision: The Development of Technique in John Wain's First Seven Novels," *South Atlantic Quarterly* 17(Summer 1969): 336.

4. *Strike the Father Dead* (New York: St. Martin's Press, 1962), p. 327. All subsequent page references in this chapter are to this edition of the novel.

5. See, for example: Anon., "After the Bombardment," *Times Literary Supplement*, March 23, 1962, p. 197; Frederick P. W. McDowell, "'The Devious Involutions of Human Character and Emotions': Reflections on Some Recent British Novels," *Wisconsin Studies in Contemporary Literature* 4(Autumn 1963): 342.

6. "Books: Pitfalls in the Search for Identity," *Commonweal* 77(October 5, 1962): 47.

7. "Living in the Present," *Manchester Guardian*, July 14, 1961, p. 5.

8. See, for example: Martin Price, "The Complexity of Awareness and the Awareness of Complexity: Some Recent Novels," *Yale Review* NS 52(Winter 1962): 266; Robert Taubman, "Trad Man," *New Statesman and Nation* 63(March 23, 1962): 419.

9. Mellown, p. 338.

10. James Gindin, "John Wain," in *Contemporary Novelists*, edited by James Vinson (New York: St Martin's Press, 1972), p. 1291.

11. Ibid.

Chapter Four

1. *Sprightly Running* (New York: St. Martin's Press, 1963), p. 234.

2. "John Wain," in *The Writer's Place: Interviews on the Literary Situation in Contemporary Britain*, edited by Peter Firchow (Minneapolis: University of Minnesota Press, 1974), p. 327.

3. Anon., "Spade Work," *Newsweek* 66(September 27, 1965): 108.

4. "John Wain," p. 326.

5. Anon., p. 108.

6. *The Young Visitors* (New York: Viking Press, 1965), p. 22. All subsequent page references in this chapter, unless otherwise identified, are to this edition of the novel.

7. Elgin W. Mellown, "Steps Toward Vision: The Development of Technique in John Wain's First Seven Novels," *South Atlantic Quarterly* 17(Summer 1969): 339.

8. "John Wain," p. 326.

9. *The Smaller Sky* (London: Penguin Books, Ltd., 1969), p. 21. All subsequent page references in this chapter are to this edition of the novel.

10. See, for example: Anon., "Dropping Out," *Times Literary Supplement*, October 5, 1967, p. 933; R. G. G. Price, "New Novels," *Punch* 253(October 11, 1967): 562.

11. "The Death of Privacy," London *Times*, October 5, 1967, p. 8.

12. "Fiction: William Trevor Sees Paddington Afresh," *Books and Bookmen* 13(October 1967): 46.

13. Michael Ratcliffe, "The Death of Privacy," London *Times*, October 5, 1967, p. 8.

14. George Clive, "New Novels: Desert Victory," *Spectator* 219(October 6, 1967): 398.

15. Gillian Freeman, "Points of Departure," *New Statesman and Nation* 74(October 6, 1967): 440.

Chapter Five

1. "Three English Novels," *Nation* 211(October 5, 1970): 313; "Fiction," *Library Journal* 95(August 1970): 2723; "Quarterly Fiction Review," *Contemporary Review* 217(July 1970): 43–44.

2. Anon., "Language and Literature: English and American," *Choice* 8(September 1971): 836; Anon., "Rebel with a Small Cause," *Times Literary Supplement*, April 30, 1970, p. 471.

3. "Setting up the Targets," London *Times Saturday Review*, May 2, 1970, p. iv.

4. *A Winter in the Hills* (New York: Viking Press, 1970), p. 227. All subsequent page references in this chapter, unless otherwise identified, are to this edition of the novel.

5. *The Pardoner's Tale* (New York: Viking Press, 1979), p. 36. All subsequent page references in this chapter, unless otherwise identified, are to this edition of the novel.

6. For a brief discussion of Chaucer parallels, see the following: Anon., "Fiction: Anger and After," *Economist*, November 18, 1978, p. 153; D. A. N. Jones, "Forty-ish and Riggish," *Times Literary Supplement*, October 13, 1978, p. 1140; Roger Flaherty, "Wain's Erotic Double Tale," *Chicago Sun-Times*, April 8, 1979, p. 34; Rob Schmieder, "Fiction," *Library Journal*, February 1, 1979, p. 421.

7. "Fiction," *Booklist*, April 1, 1979, p. 1206.

8. "Recent Fiction," *Illustrated London News* 266(December 1978): 123.

9. Julian Moynahan, "Novel in a Novel," *New York Times Book Review*, March 25, 1979, p. 15.

Chapter Six

1. "Steps Toward Vision: The Development of Technique in John Wain's First Seven Novels," *South Atlantic Quarterly*, 17(Summer 1969): 330.

2. "Plain Man of Letters," *Nation* 185(October 26, 1957): 285.

3. "A Sort of Rebels," in his *The Novel Now: A Guide to Contemporary Fiction* (New York: W. W. Norton, 1967), p. 146.

4. "Steps Toward Vision," p. 341.

5. *Nuncle and Other Stories* (New York: St. Martin's Press, 1960), p. 21. All subsequent page references in this chapter, unless otherwise identified, are to this edition of the collection.

6. H. T. K., "Books Reviewed," *Canadian Forum* 41(August 1961): 117.

7. *Death of the Hind Legs and Other Stories* (London: Penguin Books, Ltd., 1970), p. 46. All subsequent page references in this chapter, unless otherwise identified, are to this edition of the collection.

8. F. M. Kuna, "Current Literature 1971: II. New Writing: Fiction," *English Studies* 53(April 1972): 479.

9. Richard P. Brickner, "Two in the Modern Tradition," *New Leader* 55(May 15, 1972): 23.

10. Richard Quintana, "Book Reviews," *Wisconsin Studies in Contemporary Literature* 3(Winter 1962): 84.

11. *Sprightly Running: Part of an Autobiography* (New York: St. Martin's Press, 1963), p. 202.

12. W. W. Robson, "Epilogue: Literature Since 1950," in his *Modern English Literature* (London and New York: Oxford University Press, 1970), p. 154.

13. *Professing Poetry* (Middlesex, England: Penguin, 1977), p. 274.

14. Ian Fletcher, "John Wain," in *Contemporary Poets of the English Language*, edited by Rosalie Murphy (London: St. James Press; New York: St. Martin's Press, 1970), p. 1132.

15. Ibid.

16. *Weep Before God: Poems* (New York: St. Martin's Press, 1961), p. 37, ll. 10–12. All subsequent page references in this chapter, unless otherwise identified, are to this edition of the poems.

17. *Letters to Five Artists* (New York: Viking Press, 1970), p. 9. All subsequent page references in this chapter, unless otherwise identified, are to this edition of the poems.

18. *Feng: A Poem* (New York: Viking Press, 1975), p. iv. All subsequent page references in this chapter, unless otherwise identified, are to this edition of the poems.

19. *Preliminary Essays* (New York: St. Martin's Press, 1957), p. 187. All subsequent page references in this chapter, unless otherwise identified, are to this edition of the book.

20. "The Moral Center in John Wain's Fiction," in his *Postwar British Fiction: New Accents and Attitudes* (Berkeley and Los Angeles: University of California Press, 1962), p. 142.

21. "The Daughters of Earth and the Sons of Heaven: Edmund Wilson and the Word," in *Edmund Wilson: The Man and His Work*, edited by John Wain (New York: New York University Press, 1978), p. 147.

22. Ibid.

23. "Along the Tightrope," in *Declaration,* edited by Tom Maschler (New York: E. P. Dutton, 1958), p. 69.

24. "Introduction," in his *A House for the Truth* (New York: Viking Press, 1973), p. 2. All subsequent page references in this chapter, unless otherwise identified, are to this edition of the book.

25. "Foreward," in his *Professing Poetry* (London: Macmillan, 1977), p. viii. All subsequent page references in this chapter, unless otherwise identified, are to this edition of the book.

26. *Samuel Johnson* (New York: Viking Press, 1975), p. 352. All subsequent page references in this chapter, unless otherwise identified, are to this edition of the book.

27. Jim Hicks, "About John Wain," in *Book-of-the-Month Club News,* Spring 1975, p. 4.

28. Ibid.

29. Ibid.

30. Ibid.

31. "John Wain's Life of Samuel Johnson," *New York Times Book Review,* March 16, 1975, p. 7.

Selected Bibliography

PRIMARY SOURCES

1. Fiction

Hurry on Down. London: Secker and Warburg, 1953, 1978; New York: Viking Press, 1965. Published in United States as *Born in Captivity*. New York: Alfred A. Knopf, 1954.

Living in the Present. London: Secker and Warburg, 1955; New York: Putnam's, 1960.

The Contenders. London: Macmillan; New York: St. Martin's Press, 1958.

A Travelling Woman. London: Macmillan; New York: St. Martin's Press, 1959.

Nuncle and Other Stories. London: Macmillan; New York: St. Martin's Press, 1960.

Strike the Father Dead. London: Macmillan; New York: St. Martin's Press, 1962.

The Young Visitors. London: Macmillan; New York: Viking Press, 1965.

Death of the Hind Legs and Other Stories. London: Macmillan; New York: Viking Press, 1966.

The Smaller Sky. London: Macmillan, 1967.

A Winter in the Hills. London: Macmillan; New York: Viking Press, 1970.

The Life Guard: Stories. London: Macmillan, 1971; New York: Viking Press, 1972.

The Pardoner's Tale. London: Macmillan, 1978; New York: Viking Press, 1979.

2. Verse

Mixed Feelings: Nineteen Poems. Reading, Berkshire: Reading University School of Art, 1951.

A Word Carved on a Sill. London: Routledge; New York: St. Martin's Press, 1956.

Weep Before God: Poems. London: Macmillan; New York: St. Martin's Press, 1961.

A Song About Major Eatherly. Iowa City: Qara Press, 1961; reprinted in *Weep Before God*, 1961.

Wildtrack: A Poem. London: Macmillan, 1965; New York: Viking Press, 1966.

Letters to Five Artists. London: Macmillan, 1969; New York: Viking Press, 1970.
The Shape of Feng. London: Covent Garden Press, 1972.
Feng: A Poem. London: Macmillan; New York: Viking Press, 1975.
Poems: 1949-1979. London: Macmillan, 1980.

3. Other Prose
Preliminary Essays. London: Macmillan; New York: St. Martin's Press, 1957.
Gerard Manley Hopkins: An Idiom of Desperation. London: Oxford University Press; Folcroft, Pennsylvania: Folcroft Editions, 1959; reprinted in *Essays on Literature and Ideas,* 1963.
Sprightly Running: Part of an Autobiography. London: Macmillan, 1962; New York: St. Martin's Press, 1963.
Essays on Literature and Ideas. London: Macmillan; New York: St. Martin's Press, 1963.
The Living World of Shakespeare: A Playgoer's Guide. London: Macmillan; New York: St. Martin's Press, 1964.
Arnold Bennett. New York: Columbia University Press, 1967.
A House for the Truth: Critical Essays. London: Macmillan, 1972; New York: Viking Press, 1973.
Samuel Johnson. London: Macmillan, 1974, 1980; New York: Viking Press, 1975.
Professing Poetry. London: Macmillan, 1977; New York: Viking Press, 1978.

4. Editor
Contemporary Reviews of Romantic Poetry. London: Harrap; New York: Barnes and Noble, 1953.
Interpretations: Essays on Twelve English Poems. London: Routledge, 1955, 1972; New York: Hillary House, 1957.
International Literary Annual. London: John Calder, 1958, 1959; New York: Criterion Books, 1959, 1960.
Fanny Burney's Diary. London: Folio Society, 1961.
Pope. New York: Dell, 1963.
Anthology of Modern Poetry. London: Hutchinson, 1963.
Selected Shorter Poems of Thomas Hardy. London: Macmillan; New York: St. Martin's Press, 1966.
Selected Stories of Thomas Hardy. London: Macmillan; New York: St. Martin's Press, 1966.
The Dynasts. London: Macmillan, 1965; New York: St. Martin's Press, 1966.
Shakespeare: Macbeth: A Casebook. London: Macmillan, 1968.
Shakespeare: Othello: A Casebook. London: Macmillan, 1971.
Johnson as Critic. London and Boston: Routledge, 1973.

Samuel Johnson: Lives of the English Poets: A Selection. London: Dent, 1975; New York: Dutton, 1975.

Johnson on Johnson: A Selection of the Personal and Autobiographical Writings of Samuel Johnson(1709–1784). London: Dent; New York: Dutton, 1976.

Personal Choice: A Poetry Anthology. North Pomfret, Vermont: David and Charles, 1978.

An Edmund Wilson Celebration. London: Phaidon; also published as *Edmund Wilson: The Man and His Work.* New York: New York University Press, 1978.

The New Wessex Selection of Thomas Hardy's Poetry (ed. with Eirian Wain). London: Macmillan, 1978.

Anthology of Contemporary Poetry. London: Hutchinson, 1979.

5. Drama
The Take-Over Bid (radio), 1963.
The Young Visitors (television), 1967.
Dr. Johnson Out of Town (radio), 1974.
Harry in the Night: An Optimistic Comedy (stage), 1975.
Assassination (radio), 1976.
You Wouldn't Remember (radio), 1978.

6. Selected Essays and Book Reviews
"Strategy of Victorian Poetry." *Twentieth Century* 153(May 1953): 383–90.
"Servicing Shakespeare." *Twentieth Century* 154(August 1953): 141–45.
"Horizon." *Spectator,* January 15, 1954, p. 75.
"Last of George Orwell." *Twentieth Century* 155(January and March 1954): 71–78, 237–38.
"Thirties Together." *Spectator,* March 19, 1954, pp. 332–33.
"Bergmann's Masterpiece." *Spectator,* June 18, 1954, pp. 742–43.
"The Quality of Arnold Bennett." *Twentieth Century* 156(September and October 1954): 253–67, 341–57.
"Pleasure, Controversy, Scholarship." *Spectator,* October 1, 1954, pp. 403–405.
"View of the Novel." *Spectator,* October 22, 1954, pp. 500–501.
"Orwell," *Spectator,* November 19, 1954, p. 630.
"Shelleyan Aftermath." *Spectator,* December 15, 1954, pp. 790–91.
"Liberation of Wordsworth." *Twentieth Century* 157(January 1955): 66–78.
"A Kind of History." *Spectator,* February 11, 1955, pp. 159–60.
"Language of Criticism." *Spectator,* February 25, 1955, pp. 227–28.
"A Stranger and Afraid." *Spectator,* March 25, 1955, pp. 359–60.
"Riddling Days." *Spectator,* April 8, 1955, pp. 442–43.

"Who Talks of My Nation?" *Spectator*, April 29, 1955, pp. 553–54.

"Teaching of D. H. Lawrence." *Twentieth Century* 157(May 1955): 462–69.

"Pudd'nhead Wilson." *Spectator*, May 20, 1955, pp. 652–53.

"One Man, One Poem." *Spectator*, June 10, 1955, p. 747.

"Disguises of Walt Whitman." *Spectator*, June 24, 1955, pp. 802–803.

"Shakespearean Theme." *Spectator*, July 15, 1955, p. 100.

"A Daniel Comes to Judgment." *Spectator*, July 29, 1955, pp. 171–72.

"Samuel Deronda: A Summer Serial." *Spectator*, August 5 and September 9, 1955, pp. 196, 224, 255–56, 281–82, 310–11, 336–37.

"Frontiers of Civility." *Spectator*, September 16, 1955, p. 367.

"Moral, Grave, Sublime." *Spectator*, September 9, 1955, pp. 339–40.

"Beauties of Johnson." *Spectator*, September 30, 1955, pp. 422–23.

"Leavis on Lawrence." *Spectator*, October 7, 1955, pp. 457–59.

"Mind of Autolycus." *Spectator*, November 11, 1955, p. 624.

"Bruising Experience." *Spectator*, December 2, 1955, p. 770.

"Literary Critic in the University." *Twentieth Century* 159(February 1956): 142–50.

"Third Man." *Twentieth Century* 160(December 1956), 499–505.

"How It Strikes a Contemporary." *Twentieth Century* 161(March 1957): 227–36.

"A Few Drinks with Alcock and Brown." *Kenyon Review* 19(Spring 1957): 233–45.

"English Poetry: The Immediate Situation." *Sewanee Review* 65(Summer 1957): 353–74.

"Simply Heavenly." *Twentieth Century* 164(July 1958): 71–74.

"Instrument of Communication." *Times Literary Supplement*, August 15, 1958, p. 2946.

"Bring Your Own Blankets." *Twentieth Century* 164(September 1958): 269–72.

"Equity and Amateurs." *Twentieth Century* 164(October 1958): 350–54.

"Poem in Words of One Syllable." *Kenyon Review* 20(Winter 1958): 45–46.

"Chatterton Lecture on an English Poet: Gerard Manley Hopkins: An Idiom of Desperation." *Proceedings of the British Academy* 44(1959): 173–97.

"Introduction to an Autobiography." *London Magazine* 20(February 1959): 37–39.

"The Month." *Twentieth Century* 166(July 1959): 25–29.

"Shadow of An Epic." *Spectator*, March 11, 1960, p. 360.

"Jest in Season." *Twentieth Century* 167 (June 1960): 530–44.

"My Nineteen-Thirties." *Evergreen Review* 9(Summer 1960): 76–89.

"Voice from the Bath-Chair." *Twentieth Century* 168(December 1960): 508–12.

"Lost Horizons?" *Encounter* 16(January 1961): 66–71.

"A Visit to India." *Encounter* 16(May 1961): 3–15.

"Church and People in New Housing Areas." *Church Quarterly Review* 163(January–March 1962): 72–83.

"Cathedral Call." *Guardian*, March 10, 1962, p. 5.

"In the Master Class." *Guardian*, April 12, 1962, p. 7.

"The Conflict of Forms in Contemporary English Literature." *Critical Quarterly* 4(Spring 1962): 7–30.

"Australian Composer." *Guardian*, July 19, 1962, p. 6.

"Meyerstein: An Oxford Memoir." *Encounter* 19(August 1962): 27–42.

"London Letter." *Hudson Review* 15(Summer 1962; Winter 1962–63): 253–60, 586–88.

"Voluntary Service Overseas." *Guardian*, October 12, 1962, p. 16.

"Nuvolari, Meet the Soda-Pop Man." *Listener* 69(February 14, 1963): 301.

"Our Situation." *Encounter* 20 (May 1963): 3–15.

"A New Novel About Old Troubles: *Catch-22* by Joseph Heller." *Critical Quarterly* 5(Summer 1963): 168–73.

"Notes on Imagination and Judgment." *Times Literary Supplement*, July 26, 1963, p. 561.

"Guides to Shakespeare." *Encounter* 22(March 1964): 53–62.

"C. S. Lewis." *Encounter* 22(May 1964): 51–57.

"Engagement or Withdrawal? Some Notes on the Work of Philip Larkin." *Critical Quarterly* 6(Summer 1964): 167–68.

"Theodore Roethke." *Critical Quarterly* 6(Winter 1964): 322–38.

"T. S. Eliot." *Encounter* 24(March 1965): 51–53.

"Poet and Doppelgänger." *Listener*, April 29, 1965, pp. 627–29.

"The BBC's Duty to Society." *Listener*, July 15, 1965, pp. 81–82.

"Letter from Oxford: Electing a Poet." *Encounter* 26(April 1966): 51–52.

"The Poetry of Thomas Hardy." *Critical Quarterly* 8(Summer 1966): 166–73.

"MacNeice as Critic." *Encounter* 27(November 1966): 49–55.

"The Shakespearean Lie-Detector: Thoughts on *Much Ado About Nothing.*" *Critical Quarterly* 9(Spring 1967): 27–42.

" 'To Write for My Own Race': The Fiction of Flann O'Brien." *Encounter* 29(July 1967): 71–85.

"The Meaning of Dr. Zhivago." *Critical Quarterly* 10(Spring-Summer 1968): 113–37.

"Orwell and the Intelligentsia." *Encounter* 31(December 1968): 72–80.

"England." *Kenyon Review* 31(Winter 1969): 82–85.

"A Note on Ruth Pitter's Poetry." *Listener*, February 20, 1969, pp. 239-40.

"The Prophet Ezra v. 'the Egotistical Sublime': On Pound, Eliot, Joyce." *Encounter* 33(August 1969): 63-70.

"To Criticize the Critic." *Encounter* 33(November 1969): 75-87.

"Art, If You Like." *Encounter* 34(May 1970): 68-71.

"The Coronation of the Novel." *Listener*, June 4, 1970, p. 755.

"Salade Nicoise." *Encounter* 35(August 1970): 39-43.

"The Disappearing Critic." *Listener*, August 6, 1970, pp. 165-67.

"A Salute to the Makers." *Encounter* 35(November 1970): 51-59.

"Radio till Now: Between Culture and Kitsch." *Encounter* 36(June 1971): 61-65.

"The New Puritanism, the New Academicism, the New, the New. . . ." *Critical Quarterly* 14(Spring 1972): 8-18.

"Dr. Johnson as Poet." *Encounter* 39 (May 1972): 53.

"The Single Mind: A Review of Lionel Trilling: *Sincerity and Authenticity.*" *Critical Quarterly* 15(Summer 1973): 173-79.

"Swing High, Swing Low: Reflections on a Saturday Night Out." *Encounter* 41(July 1973): 3-12.

"Auden: Poet of Opposites." *Observer*, September 30, 1973, p. 39.

"Writing in the Seventies: Letter to the Editor." *Author* 83(Winter 1973): 157-59.

"Alternative Poetry: An Oxford Inaugural Lecture." *Encounter* 42(June 1974): 26-38.

"Homage to Emily Dickinson" *Carleton Miscellany* 15(Fall-Winter 1974-75): 2-17.

"What It Means to Me." *Observer*, June 1, 1975, p. 9.

"On the Breaking of Forms." *Encounter* 45(August 1975): 49-56.

"Poetry and Social Criticism: Should Poets Try to Change the World." *Encounter* 46(June 1976): 25-33.

"This Is Your Scholar! Your Philosopher." *Transactions of the Johnson Society* 33(December 1976): 5-20.

"Reflections on the First Night of *Comus.*" *Encounter* 48(March 1977): 33-42.

"Just the Ticket." *Observer*, April 23, 1978, p. 13.

SECONDARY SOURCES

ALLEN, WALTER. "War and Post War: British," in his *Tradition and Dream: The English and American Novel from the Twenties to*

Our Time. London: Phoenix House, 1964, pp. 278–82. Compares the early works of Wain, Iris Murdoch, and Kingsley Amis.

ALVAREZ, A. "Poetry of the Fifties: In England." *International Literary Annual,* No. 1. Edited by John Wain. London: John Calder, 1958, pp. 97–107. Informative survey of the development of the poetic "Movement" in the 1950s.

BLUESTONE, GEORGE. "John Wain and John Barth: The Angry and the Accurate." *Massachusetts Review* 1(May 1960): 582–86, 589. Memoir of Wain's speech at the University of Washington in 1959. Comments on the novels through *A Travelling Woman.*

BODE, CARL. "The Redbrick Cinderellas." *College English* 20(April 1959): 332, 334–37. Discusses Wain's early novels and criticism; concludes that Wain's conservatism affects all of his writings.

BURGESS, ANTHONY. "A Sort of Rebels," in his *The Novel Now: A Guide to Contemporary Fiction.* New York: W. W. Norton, 1967, pp. 144–46, 149–53. Discusses some of the strengths and weaknesses of Wain's novels through *The Young Visitors.*

DUECK, JACK. "Uses of the Picaresque: A Study of Five Modern British Novels." Ph.D. dissertation. University of Notre Dame, 1973. A detailed examination of the picaresque elements in *Hurry on Down.*

FIRCHOW, PETER, ed. "John Wain," in his *The Writer's Place: Interviews on the Literary Situation in Contemporary Britain.* Minneapolis: University of Minnesota Press, 1974, pp. 313–330. Interview with Wain, offering his views on the social role of the professional serious writer in contemporary Britain.

FRASER, G. S. *The Modern Writer and His World.* Baltimore: Penguin Books, 1964, 427 pp. passim. Considers the differences and similarities between the writings of Wain and Amis.

GERARD, DAVID. *My Work as a Novelist: John Wain.* Cardiff: Drake Educational Associates, 1978. Taped interview with Wain covering the evolution of his novels from *Hurry on Down* to *A Winter in the Hills.* He also deals with his role as Oxford Professor of Poetry from 1973–1978.

GERARD, MARTIN. "Goodbye to All That: A Child's Guide to Two Decades." *X, A Quarterly Review* 1(November 1959): 114–20. Tries to make some sense of the "Movement" poets.

GINDIN, JAMES J. "Comedy in Contemporary British Fiction." *Papers of the Michigan Academy of Science, Arts, and Letters.* Vol. 44. Edited by Sheridan Baker. Ann Arbor: University of Michigan Press, 1959, pp. 389–91, 395–97. Wain's novels fit in with the major traditions of the eighteenth- and nineteenth-century English novel.

————. "John Wain," in *Contemporary Novelists*. Edited by James Vinson. New York: St. Martin's Press, 1972, pp. 1289-93. Discusses Wain's developing themes, comedy, characterization, and structure.

————. "The Moral Center of John Wain's Fiction," in his *Postwar British Fiction: New Accents and Attitudes*. Berkeley and Los Angeles: University of California, 1962, pp. 128-44. Examines Wain's first four novels and his collection of short stories, and finds that through them runs a constant commitment to the "moral worth of the individual."

————. "The Reassertion of the Personal." *Texas Quarterly* 4(Fall 1958): 126-34. The fairy-tale endings to the novels of Wain, Amis, and Angus Wilson signify a great difference from comic novels of a generation ago.

————. "Well Beyond Laughter: Directions from Fifties' Comic Fiction." *Studies in the Novel* 3(Winter 1971): 357-58, 362-64. Examines the "comic iconoclasm" in the works of Wain and his contemporaries.

HAMILTON, IAN. "The Making of the Movement." *New Statesman* 81(April 23, 1971): 570-71. The Movement was a "concerted reaction against the tangled and pretentious neoromanticism of the postwar years."

HARKNESS, BRUCE. "The Lucky Crowd—Contemporary British Fiction." *English Journal* 47(October 1958): 387-92, 395-97. Finds similarities in characterization, style, and thematic content in the novels of Wain and Amis.

HARVEY, W. T. "Have You Anything to Declare? or, Angry Young Men: Facts and Fiction." *International Literary Annual*, No. 1. Edited by John Wain. London: John Calder, 1958, pp. 47-59. Studies the origins and development of the Angry Young Men myth.

HEPPENSTALL, RAYNER. "They Like It Here," in his *The Fourfold Tradition: Notes on the French and English Literatures*. London: Barrie and Rockliff, 1961, pp. 213-20, 244-46. Discusses the "Wain-Amis phenomenon" during the 1950s with an analysis of each writer's first four novels.

HOLLOWAY, JOHN. "'Tank in the Stalls': Notes on the 'School of Anger,'" in his *The Charted Mirror: Literary and Critical Essays*. London: Routledge and Kegan Paul, 1960, pp. 142-44. Examines Wain's verse as a way of coming to terms with the Angry Young Men phenomenon.

JENNINGS, ELIZABETH. "Poetry of the Fifties," in her *Let's Have Some Poetry!* London: Museum Press, 1960, pp. 96-97, 103. Finds a heavy influence of Empson on Wain's verse.

KARL, F. R. "The Angries: Is There a Protestant in the House?" in his *A Reader's Guide to the Contemporary English Novel.* New York: Farrar, Straus and Giroux, 1962, 304 pp. passim. Wain's novels, together with those of many of his contemporaries, suggest a "narrow range, superficial analyses, irresponsible and aimless protagonists, anti-heroic acts, anti-intellectualism, and slapstick comedy."

LEHMANN, JOHN. "The Wain-Larkin Myth." *Sewanee Review* 66(Autumn 1958): 578-87. Seeks to explain why Wain's views on the development of English poetry are wrong.

MELLOWN, ELGIN W. "Steps Toward Vision: The Development of Technique in John Wain's First Seven Novels." *South Atlantic Quarterly* 17(Summer 1969): 330-42. Focuses on the development of Wain's narrative technique as offering the most positive evidence of his potential growth.

MOORE, GEOFFREY. "Poets of the Fifties," in his *Poetry Today.* London: Longmans for British Council, 1958, pp. 45-51. Discusses the Movement Poets' manifesto and its origins.

MORGAN, W. JOHN. "Authentic Voices." *Twentieth Century* 161(February 1957): 32-34. Examines the origins of the Angry Young Men and the poetic Movement.

O'CONNOR, WILLIAM VAN. "John Wain: The Will to Write." *Wisconsin Studies in Contemporary Literature* 1(Winter 1960): 35-49. Discusses Wain's career as it relates to his novels, poetry, and criticism. In all three genres, Wain's search for a subject has been toward "old-fashioned moral truths."

PESCHMANN, HERMAN. "The Nonconformists: Angry Young Men, 'Lucky Jims,' and 'Outsiders.'" *English* (London) 13(Winter 1960): 14. Wain shows "a discriminating traditionalism and a recognition of certain elements in the social and education system which, without finding them wholly admirable, he accepts as answering a deep-rooted need."

RIES, LAWRENCE R. "John Wain: The Evasive Answer," in his *Wolf Masks: Violence in Contemporary Poetry.* New York, London: Kennikat Press, pp. 130-43. Examines Wain's role as spokesman for the neohumanistic position in his poetry and criticism.

SALWAK, DALE. *John Braine and John Wain: A Reference Guide.* Boston: G. K. Hall, 1980. Annotated listing of the secondary criticism of Wain's works. Includes a discussion of the development of his literary reputation.

SCOTT, GEORGE. "Jolly Jack and Lucky Jim," in his *Time and Place.* London: Staples Press, 1956, pp. 215-17. Finds several similarities in the works of Amis, Wain, and Murdoch.

STANFORD, DEREK. "Beatniks and Angry Young Men." *Meanjin* 17(Summer 1958): 413, 417-19. Both Wain and Braine are "mesmerically possessed by the theme of careerism" and are critical, by implication, of the psychology of their characters.

TYNAN, KENNETH. "The Men of Anger." *Holiday* 23(April 1958): 117, 181-82. Surveys the development of the Angry Young Men.

VALENCIA, WILLA F. "The Picaresque Tradition in the Contemporary English and American Novel." Ph.D. dissertation. University of Illinois, 1968. Analyzes Wain's early novels and finds them faithful to the historical picaresque tradition.

WALZER, MICHAEL. "John Wain: The Hero in Limbo." *Perspective* 10(Summer-Autumn 1958): 137-45. Finds in Wain's first three novels a clear presentation of a new picaresque hero.

WEAVER, ROBERT. "England's Angry Young Men—Mystics, Provincials and Radicals." *Queen's Quarterly* 65(Summer 1958): 185, 188-90. Groups together Wain, Amis, and Braine as "provincial" Angry Young Men—in contrast to "mystics" (Wilson, Holroyd, and Hopkins)and "radicals" (Osborne, Tynan, and Anderson).

WILSON, COLIN. "The Writer and Publicity." *Encounter* 13(November 1959): 9. Considers the case history of *Hurry on Down* as a way of showing that today, in literary England, the writer's personality is involved in promotion.

YVARD, P. "Literature and Society in the Fifties in Great Britain." *Journal of European Studies* 3(March 1973): 36-37, 39-40. Wain, Amis, Braine, and Osborne show that literature can have a social, moral, and even metaphysical impact on a "disturbed postwar audience" at a time when most traditional values were already being challenged.

Index